FREE STUFF FOR KIDS

Edited by Maureen Maddren

OUR PLEDGE

We have collected the best offers — either free or very
cheap — that we could find. We have examined every
single item. We don't think you'll be disappointed when
you send away for things (though mistakes do happen)
because every supplier of items in this book has promised,
in writing, to honour single requests.

EXLEY

Our heartfelt appreciation goes to the hundreds of charities, companies and organisations for their cooperation in making this book possible. We also want to thank the children who have given us their own ideas for FREE STUFF. The suppliers and publishers of this book have a common goal – to make it possible for children to reach out and discover the world by themselves.

The first UK edition published in 1981 by
Exley Publications Ltd,
16 Chalk Hill, Watford, Herts WD1 4BN, United Kingdom.

This 9th edition copyright © Exley Publications, 1989

British Library Cataloguing in Publication Data

Free stuff for kids. —— 9th ed.
   1. Free material. Lists – For children.
   I. Title.
   011′.03
ISBN 1-85015-153-9 (h/b)
ISBN 1-85015-154-7 (p/b)

We would like to thank all those who have supplied us with illustrations for their entries. Additional illustrations supplied by Mike Scott.

Typeset by Brush Off Studios, St Albans, Herts.
Printed and bound in Hungary.

what's inside

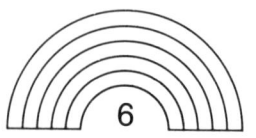

about this book

FREE STUFF FOR KIDS contains over 250 things that children can send away for. We think the items in this book are the best fun offers available to children. You will not find any "trick" offers – only wholesome, safe, fun and informative things we know kids like!

As costs keep rising it is not surprising that some items require a small fee or stamped addressed envelope. In this edition we have allowed a charge of up to, but not more than, £2.00 excluding postage. We would like all the things offered in the book to be free but because we have received some really good inexpensive offers it seemed a pity not to include those as well. Of course, there is still plenty of free stuff in the book so, apart from occasionally sending the cost of postage, you do not *have* to spend anything at all!

We have examined every item in this book. Each supplier of items has agreed in writing to honour single requests until July 1991.

The book is designed especially for independent use by children who can read and write. General directions in the introductory pages explain exactly how to send a request. Postal instructions for each item are clear and consistent. Half the fun is knowing you can use the book entirely on your own. The other half is getting a real reward for your efforts.

using this book

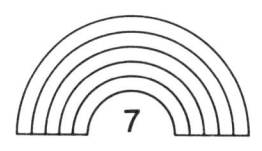

reading carefully

Read all the descriptions carefully so you will know exactly what you are getting. Is it a leaflet or a booklet? A map or a poster? A catalogue or a magazine?

using the index

If you want posters for your room then look up 'posters' in the index which starts on page 117. You can also look up other things that interest you, like stamps, photography, dolls or games.

following directions

Make sure you follow the directions for each thing you send for. Most often the directions will tell you to use a postcard. Sometimes you will need to use paper and an envelope.

waiting

You should expect to wait 2 to 5 weeks for your things to arrive. We know it is a long time to wait. But if your things come sooner (and many of them will), then it will be a nice surprise.

sending postcards

Your postcard should look like this. The date, the request and your address are on one side. The company's address and the stamp are on the other side.

The British Gas
Education Service
PO Box 46
Hounslow,
Middx. TW4 6NF

19 Swan Road
Some town
Lincolnshire
4 May 1989
Dear Sir or Madam,
Please send me the
Energy House snakes and
ladders game.
Thank you very much.
Yours faithfully,
Jane Rogers

sending letters

Your letter should look like this one. If you are enclosing stamps, a cheque, a postal order or a stamped addressed envelope, say so in the letter.

Ask for only one copy.
- Print the name of the thing you want exactly as you see it in the directions.
- Print the complete address of the company exactly as you see it in the directions.
- Print your own name, street, town, county and postcode very carefully.

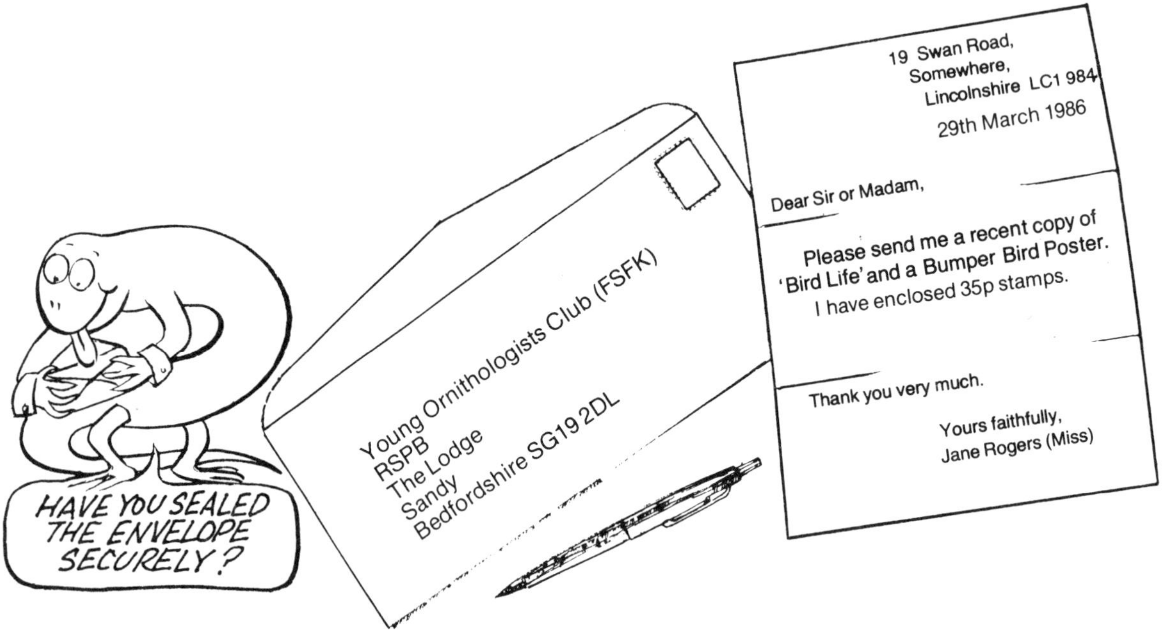

HAVE YOU SEALED THE ENVELOPE SECURELY?

Young Ornithologists Club (FSFK)
RSPB
The Lodge
Sandy
Bedfordshire SG19 2DL

19 Swan Road,
Somewhere,
Lincolnshire LC1 984
29th March 1986

Dear Sir or Madam,

Please send me a recent copy of 'Bird Life' and a Bumper Bird Poster. I have enclosed 35p stamps.

Thank you very much.

Yours faithfully,
Jane Rogers (Miss)

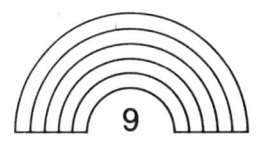

enclosing money

Most firms ask you to pay very small amounts (say, under 30p) by enclosing stamps in your letter. This is to save people the trouble of getting a postal order or sending a cheque. Don't stick the stamps to your paper but do mention in your letter that you've enclosed them.

If you are not asked to pay with stamps then you must enclose a postal order or a cheque. To send a postal order go to your post office and they will tell you what you have to do. Or, Mum or Dad could make out a cheque.

If the directions say to send a coin, it's best to sellotape the coin to your letter so it won't break out of your envelope.

sending a stamped addressed envelope (s.a.e.)

If the directions say that you should enclose a stamped addressed envelope, here's how you do it. First address an envelope to yourself. Put a second-class stamp on it. Then fold it up and put it inside another envelope with your letter. Finally, address the second envelope to the company and put a second-class stamp on it.

double checking

- Did you follow all the directions for the things you want?
- Did you print the exact names of the things you want?
- Is your own address complete and correct?
- Is the company's whole address on your postcard or envelope?
- Is your printing neat enough to read? (Ask a friend to read it back to you if you aren't sure.)
- Don't forget to post your letters!

HAVE YOU READ THE DIRECTIONS CAREFULLY?

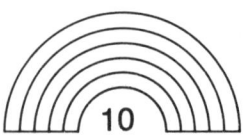

points to remember

We've tried to make the directions for using this book as clear as possible, because we want you to get what you send for. But you must follow **all** the instructions exactly as they're written on each page. If you don't it's possible that the supplier will not be able to answer your request.

Here's a list of things to remember when asking for free stuff.

- **Do not** ask for more than **one** copy of an item unless you are asked to do so.

- **Do** print your name and address clearly on the envelope **and** on the letter you send. Sometimes envelopes and letters get separated from one another.

- **Do** send all of the money asked for. Sometimes you will be asked for extra money for 'p&p'. This stands for postage and packing so you must add this charge on to the cost of the items you are ordering.

- **Do** send a stamped addressed envelope if instructions say to.

- **Do** remember to use the Postcode.

- **Do** seal the envelope securely.

- **Do not** ask Exley Publications to send you any of the items described in the book. We don't have supplies of them.

We don't want you to be disappointed, so please follow these rules.

DON'T SEND COINS OR STAMPS UNLESS YOU ARE ASKED TO DO SO.

FREE STUFF
FOR KIDS

EXLEY PUBLICATIONS

HAVE FUN

keep your pets happy

Is your cat purr-fectly happy? Cats make few demands on their owners but they must be kept properly fed and groomed. *Keeping a cat* and *A first kitten* will give you all the information you need to keep your cat contented. And there are leaflets for dog owners, too.

If you don't already own a pet, but are thinking of getting one, then the *Are you prepared?* pack will help you choose your pet.

directions: Use paper and an envelope. Enclose 14p stamp for up to 3 leaflets or 22p if you want 4 or more. Enclose £1.00 if you want the *Are you prepared?* pack.

ask for: Keeping a cat, A first kitten; Keeping a dog; Feeding your dog; The new puppy and your responsibility; Pets in summer; Training a young dog; Pets and holidays; Are animals safe in your garden?
(All leaflets are free)
Are you prepared? pack (£1.00)

write to: Information Dept (FS) (for the leaflets) OR AYP Dept (FS) (for the Are You Prepared pack)
People's Dispensary for Sick Animals
PDSA House
South Street
Dorking, Surrey RH4 2LB

fishkeeping is fun

Fish make ideal pets, they are fun to keep, relaxing to watch and provide the whole family with a hobby they can enjoy, whatever the age.

Fish are easy to care for and quite inexpensive to keep. Not surprisingly, fish have been kept for hundreds of years as pets. In fact, the Chinese, well-known for their love of fish, have been breeding goldfish for some 1600 years.

Fishkeeping Made Easy is a free guide designed to help fishkeepers, both new and old, gain more enjoyment from their hobby by providing advice on the essential aspects of this soothing pastime.

directions: Use a postcard

ask for: Fishkeeping Made Easy

write to: Dr David Ford
Aquarian Advisory Service
Thomas's
Oakwell Way
Birstall, Batley
W. Yorkshire WF17 9LU

fur, feathers and fins

Whether your pet is an angel fish or an Airedale, a budgie or a Burmese cat, these free leaflets from Pedigree Petfoods will tell you how to look after it. There is also a leaflet on feeding wild birds.

directions: Use a postcard

ask for: A code of conduct for pet owners
Pets are good for people
First aid for your dog and cat
Health and dietary care for cats & kittens
Understanding your cat's behaviour
Toilet training for dogs
Dogs in the countryside
Feeding your dog
Basic steps in dog training
Making fish feel at home
Caring for budgerigars
Looking after wild birds

write to: Pedigree Petfoods Education Centre
PO Box 77
Freepost
Burton on Trent
DE11 7BR

IS YOUR ENVELOPE ADDRESSED CORRECTLY?

popular pets

Did you know that ten million households in this country have pets but the other ten million do not. The free poster, *Twelve Steps to Good Pet Care,* will show you the best way to look after your special pet.

Now, is a Lhasa Apso a cat or a dog and what about an Egyptian Mau Smoke? You could probably guess, though, that a Full Circular Crested Light Green is a budgerigar. All these and many more dogs, cats and budgies are colourfully illustrated on wallcharts that cost just 50p each.

directions: Use a postcard (it's Freepost, so no stamp required) for the free poster, or write a letter enclosing 50p for each wallchart that you want.

ask for: Twelve Steps to Good Pet Care (free)
Popular Dogs of the World (50p)
Popular Cats of the World (50p)
Colourful World of Budgerigars (50p)

write to: Pedigree Petfoods Education Centre
PO Box 77
Freepost
Burton on Trent
DE11 7BR

pets' corner

Gerbils, mice, rabbits, hamsters, guinea-pigs and birds are fun to watch as they nibble their food or play in their cages. But all of them need special care. Find out the facts with these special leaflets.

directions: Use paper and an envelope. Enclose 14p stamp for up to 3 leaflets or 22p stamp if you want 4 or more.

ask for: The leaflet or leaflets you want from the following list: Keeping a Canary, Keeping a Budgerigar, Keeping an Aquarium, Keeping a Rabbit, Keeping a Hamster, Keeping a Guinea Pig, Keeping a Gerbil, Keeping Rats and Mice, Keeping a Parrot, Keeping a Terrapin, Keeping a Ferret.

write to: Information Department (FS)
People's Dispensary for Sick Animals
PDSA House
South Street
Dorking
Surrey RH4 2LB

what's that dog?

Can you tell a Fox Terrier from an Irish Terrier or a Basset Hound from a Blood Hound? With this chart from the National Canine Defence League you'll soon become an expert. The N.C.D.L. is Britain's leading charity for stray dogs and you can help the League by buying one of their Fun Bugs, too. With big, rolling eyes and little feet, Fun Bugs make wonderful friends. And they don't need feeding either! You can also send for a pen and a badge.

directions: Use paper and an envelope. Enclose 85p for the chart, 50p for the Fun Bug, 80p for the Pen, 25p for the Badge plus 20p postage and packing.

ask for: Dog Parade Chart (85p)
Fun Bug (50p)
N.C.D.L. Pen (80p)
N.C.D.L. Badge (25p)

write to: N.C.D.L. Promotions/ FS
1 & 2 Pratt Mews
London NW1 0AD

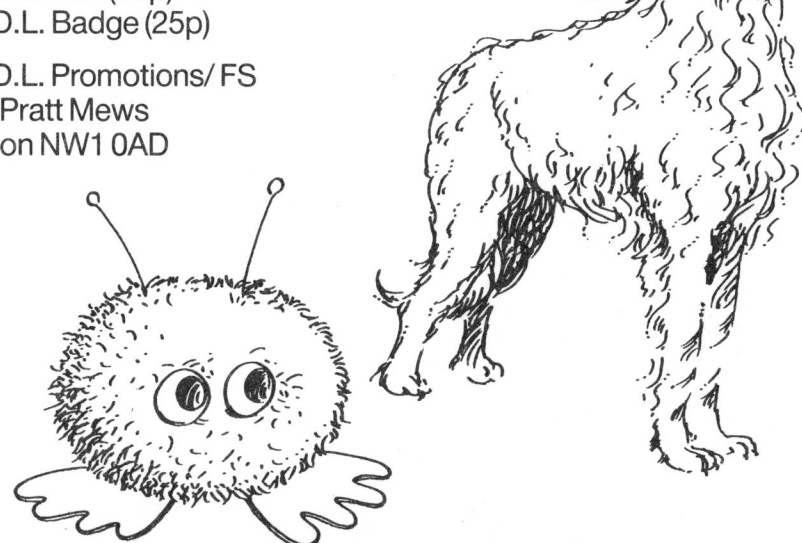

your pal for life

These three large full-colour wall charts give you facts about dogs, hints on looking after them and also show you how important they are to people. You can buy the posters individually for 75p, or the set of three is at the reduced price of £2.00.

directions: Use paper and an envelope. Enclose the correct money.

ask for: Set of 3 posters: The Dog – Your Pal For Life (£2.00) OR Dog Facts (75p); Dogs and People (75p); Dog Care (75p)

write to: Pedigree Petfoods Education Centre (FS) PO Box 77, FREEPOST (no stamp required) Burton on Trent DE11 7BR

pet care

Before you buy a pet cat or dog it is wise to find out more about how to look after it. These free leaflets will provide information on breeds, feeding, training, health and many other aspects of pet care that you will need to know.

directions: Use paper and an envelope. Enclose a stamped 9″ x 6″ envelope.

ask for: Know about Dogs
Know about Puppies
Know about Cats

write to: Spillers Foods Ltd.
Pet Advisory Dept., PO Box 221
Cambridge CB1 2SF

make friends with the coin kid

Coin collecting is a really fun hobby! It's easy to start and it needn't cost a lot – just pick out the interesting coins from the change in your pocket or the money you bring back from any foreign holiday. Very soon you'll have a collection you can really be proud of.

So if you like coin collecting, you'll love the Royal Mint Young Collectors' Club. When you join, you'll receive a super badge, an issue of the Royal Mint's Bulletin, a fantastic Young Collectors' Club medal specially struck at the Mint and exclusive to the club, and the superb colour newsletter four times a year.

Happy collecting!

directions: Use paper and an envelope. To join the club for 2 years send a crossed cheque or postal order for £1.50 made payable to the Royal Mint.

ask for: Young Coin Collectors' Club membership.

write to: Young Collectors Club
FREEPOST
P.O. Box 502
Cardiff CF1 1YY

hobby horse club

Have you ever seen Morris Dancers, Garland Dancers, Clog Dancers or Sword Dancers performing in the streets near where you live? They always have a large crowd of people around them attracted by both the music and people dressed in colourful costumes. The dancers are almost certainly members of the English Folk Dance and Song Society and now you can join the junior branch which is for under 13s and is called the Hobby Horse Club of England. As a member you get a member's badge, a current year badge, three issues of the Hobby Horse Magazine a year and a greetings card on your birthday. You will be told of all the festivals, gatherings and children's activities to be held throughout the year and of the summer holidays organised by the Hobby Horse club. Send now for details and a copy of the magazine.

directions: Use paper and an envelope. Send a stamped self-addressed envelope.

ask for: Details of the Hobby Horse Club plus a magazine.

write to: The Hobby Horse Club of England
38 Howick Cross Lane
Penwortham
Preston, Lancs PR1 0NS

chess champs

If you enjoy playing chess why not send for these three offers?
The badge usually costs 95p and the chess score book 90p,
so you'll be getting them for half price.

directions: Use paper and an envelope. Enclose a
10" x 7" 30p s.a.e. plus 95p in stamps.

ask for: Chess score book for 50 games, Badge
and Chess Press Magazine.

write to: Brian Eley & Co., FSFK offer
Dearne Road
Bolton-on-Dearne, Rotherham S63 8JR

keep on strumming

If you're just learning to play the guitar this chart could help
you to develop and keep the correct hand and finger positions.
It also has a brief history of the guitar and notes on how to
tune the strings. You could put it on your wall as a useful
memory aid.

directions: Use paper and an envelope. Enclose
postal order or cheque for 85p.

ask for: The Classical Guitar wallchart

write to: Chimera
64 High Street, Cumnor
Oxford OX2 9QD

junior casting

Prince August casting kits enable you to cast detailed figures of your choice from low melting point metal. Easy to follow instructions and hints on expanding your hobby are contained in this exciting handbook, which also has details on starter kits available. With over 100 moulds to choose from, including Napoleonic and Irish Wild Geese soldiers, fantasy monsters and characters, chess sets and a range of animals including dogs and horses, there is something for everyone. The moulds are guaranteed for 500 castings and Prince August Moulds will send you a mould of your choice, a sample figure and a 38-page colour handbook for the special price to FREE STUFF readers of £2.00.

Sample moulds available: Napoleonic soldier, fantasy character or horse.

directions: Use paper and an envelope. Send your name and address together with £2.00 in stamps, money order or cheque.

ask for: Sample figure, mould and 38-page handbook. State your choice of mould clearly.

write to: Prince August Ltd. Dept. F
Macroom, Co. Cork, Ireland.

start with stamps

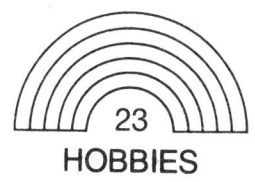
If you'd like to start collecting stamps but don't know how to
begin, this kit is definitely for you. You get these fourteen
different items absolutely free: 'Howden Junior' stamp album,
magnifier, swap holder packets, perforation gauge, watermark
detector, stamp tweezers, stamp identifier, land finder map,
packet of hinges, world's rarest stamp facsimile, school stamp
club leaflet, price list, 175 flag stamps (stickers) and a packet
of stamps.

In addition, you will be sent a collection of 'on approval'
stamps which you can buy or return. But you MUST remember
to return the 'approval' stamps if you don't want them or you
will be charged for them.

directions: Use paper and an envelope. Enclose a
14p stamp for reply postage.

ask for: The Complete Stamp Collecting Outfit
for Beginners and stamps 'on approval'

write to: Philatelic Services (Dept FSFK 1)
Eastrington
Goole
N. Humberside DN14 7QG

win a prize

The Universal Stamp Company will send you 25 different world-wide stamps free for each correct answer to the questions below. But if you answer all four correctly you will get a packet of 150, plus copies of a block of six 1840 'Penny Blacks' and a copy of a 'Penny Black' on its original envelope. In addition, you will be sent a collection of 'on approval' stamps which you can buy or return. But you MUST remember to return the 'approval' stamps if you don't want them or you will be charged for them.

Your prizes, though, are absolutely FREE whether you buy any of the stamps sent to you 'on approval' or not. You will also receive a free catalogue for all Great Britain stamps. Answer these questions:

1. What country puts ESPAÑA on its stamps?
2. Was the British PENNY BLACK the first stamp?
3. Must a stamp be postmarked to be genuine?
4. Do Irish stamps have EIRE on them?

directions: Use paper and an envelope. Write your answers clearly, include your name and address and send to the address below.

write to: Universal Stamp Company
Dept FSFK 6
Eastrington
Goole
N. Humberside DN14 7QG

let's collect stamps

This world-famous stamp company will help you to get started on a new hobby by sending you, free, a booklet called *Enjoy Stamp Collecting,* a packet of assorted stamps and a badge.

directions: Use paper and an envelope. Please enclose an extra large self-addressed envelope stamped with ·30p.

ask for: Enjoy Stamp Collecting booklet, badge, small packet of assorted stamps.

write to: Stanley Gibbons Publications Ltd
Dept FSK, 5 Parkside
Christchurch Road
Ringwood, Hants BH24 3SH

cultivating cacti

If you've ever thought about collecting cacti there's a society that can help you. It has over 100 branches in the UK where talks are held giving advice and information on growing these fascinating plants. As a member you would receive a journal four times a year, help with any problems, news about outings and shows plus an opportunity to make new friends who also enjoy growing cacti.

directions: Use paper and an envelope. Enclose a first class stamp.

ask for: Membership details

write to: Miss W E Dunn (Dept EP)
43 Dewar Drive, Sheffield S7 2GR

get stuck on stamps

Stamp collecting can be great fun and to prove it here is the Stamp Bug Club. When you join the club you get a great club badge, super membership card, special Stamp Bug Album and calendar plus a set of stickers. But best of all, every other month you'll get a copy of Stamp Bug News, full of news, information and all sorts of articles about stamp collecting. Plus in each issue there's a really useful 'Swap Special' section listing who wants to swap what for what. So if you're stuck on stamps, there's only one thing to do, join the Stamp Bug Club!

directions: Use paper and an envelope. Enclose a postal order or crossed cheque for £1.50, made payable to The Stamp Bug Club.

ask for: Stamp Bug Club membership for 2 years.

write to: Stamp Bug Club (K.S.)
FREEPOST
Northampton
NN3 1BR

HAVE YOU SEALED THE ENVELOPE SECURELY?

ice hockey

Ice hockey is a fast and furious sport enjoyed by both players and spectators alike. To help enthusiasts get even more out of the sport there is a magazine *Ice Hockey World* and a 160-page Ice Hockey Annual and for just 65p you can have a copy of both!

directions: Use paper and an envelope. Enclose your name and address and 65p in stamps.

ask for: Ice Hockey World
The Ice Hockey Annual

write to: The British Ice Hockey Association
1st Floor Suite, Merlin House
36 Southbourne Grove
Bournemouth BH6 3RA

what is netball?

In England alone over 1,000,000 school children and about 60,000 adults play netball. If you would like to know more about the game and the Netball Association write now for the fact sheet. You also get a full-colour action poster, two button badges and a sew-on badge.

directions: Use paper and an envelope. Enclose a cheque or postal order for £1.25

ask for: Fact sheet; Poster; 2 button badges; 1 sew-on badge

write to: All England Netball Association
Francis House, Francis Street
London SW1P 1DE

pot perfect, pot black

Want to know more about snooker and billiards? Here are two little booklets on the rules of the games. If you want individual tuition, the Billiards and Snooker Control Council can arrange for you to be coached for a nominal fee at one of the many centres around the country.

directions: Use paper and an envelope. Please enclose a large stamped addressed envelope, plus £1.25 for each booklet.

ask for: Snooker rules booklet (£1.25)
Billiards rules booklet (£1.25)
Guide for young players (large s.a.e.)

write to: The Development Officer
The Billiards and Snooker Control Council
Coronet House
Queen Street, Leeds LS1 2TN

land a whopper

Illustrated in this guide are thousands of different items for sea, coarse and game fishing. It makes interesting reading for all budding anglers.

directions: Use paper and an envelope. Enclose £1.00

ask for: Mullarkey & Sons' Anglers Tackle Guide

write to: Mullarkey & Sons (Free Stuff for Kids)
184/185 Waterloo Street
Burton-on-Trent, Staffs DE14 2NH

British baseball

You probably all know how popular baseball is in the United States of America, but do you also know that the *British* Baseball Federation is nearly 100 years old. The sport is now growing in popularity in this country and you can find out more about the game by writing for the fact sheet.

directions: Use paper and an envelope. Enclose 1st or 2nd class stamp.

ask for: Baseball fact sheet

write to: British Baseball Federation
East Park Lido
Hull HU8 9AW

card sports

Here's a special offer for readers of this book: soccer, cricket and tennis card games at just over half price. Follow your favourite sport with these easy-to-play card games.

directions: Use paper and an envelope. Please send £1 for each game (includes postage).

ask for: K Soccer, K Cricket or K Tennis

write to: Kentalong Ltd. (Dept. E), Longford House
25/27 Mount Ephraim Road
Tunbridge Wells, Kent TN4 8AE

how to be top

How do you get to the top in your chosen sport? A first step might be to write to the National organisations concerned to see what help is available. The following associations have all agreed to send information to Free Stuff readers on their own particular sports.

Cycle speedway

directions: Use paper and an envelope. Enclose 10" x 7" addressed envelope stamped with 24p.

ask for: The Cycle Speedway Council Handbook
Beginners' Guide to Cycle Speedway
An Introduction to Cycle Speedway

write to: Cycle Speedway Council
57 Rectory Lane, Poringland
Norwich NR14 7SW

Basketball

directions: Use paper and an envelope. Enclose 30p in stamps.

ask for: General basketball literature, Basketball stickers, a free issue of Basketball Magazine, NBA Star poster and a coaching booklet.

write to: English Basketball Association
Dept FS2 Calomax House
Lupton Avenue
Leeds LS9 7EE

Archery

directions: Use paper and an envelope. Enclose a self-addressed envelope.

ask for: Free leaflet about the Society

write to: Grand National Archery Society
7th Street, NAC Stoneleigh
Kenilworth, Warwickshire CV8 2LG

Swimming

directions: Use paper and an envelope. Enclose a 10½" x 8½" stamped addressed envelope (26p).

ask for: Awards Poster

write to: 'Free Lit. Dept'
Amateur Swimming Association
Harold Fern House, Derby Square
Loughborough, Leics LE11 0AL

Rowing

directions: Use paper and an envelope. Enclose £1.60 plus 30p postage & packing.

ask for: Learning to Row for Children

write to: Amateur Rowing Association
6 Lower Mall, London W6 9DJ

football fans take note

A FREE Promotional Pack of Football Programmes (worth £2.50) and a Catalogue which lists thousands of mint condition programmes available (all reduced in price, including Finals, Semis, Internationals and League Teams etc).

directions: Use paper and an envelope. Please enclose 50p in unused stamps for postage and packing.

ask for: Free Programmes and Catalogue

write to: Steve Earl Football Programmes (KS)
Broad Street
Bungay, Suffolk NR35 1AH

horse sense

The Pony Club publishes lots of different booklets which are helpful to young riders, and holds working rallies, film shows, summer camps and mounted expeditions.

directions: Use paper and an envelope. Enclose the correct money (£1.75 each) if you want one of the wallcharts.

ask for: Pony Club membership details
List of Pony Club books
Wallcharts 1. Tack (£1.75)
2. Grooming (£1.75)

write to: The Pony Club, British Equestrian Centre
Stoneleigh, Kenilworth
Warwickshire CV8 2LR

balloons

Balloons are fun for people of all ages. They can form the base for a papier mâché head or they can decorate the house for a party. You can even deliver a small gift to a friend by inserting the gift into the balloon and blowing it up. The Kite and Balloon Company of London prints 30 million balloons a year and is happy to give away printed samples to the readers of FREE STUFF. If you would like printed balloons with your own name on for a party they would also be pleased to help, but of course there will be a charge. Write for your free balloon samples and, if you would like specially printed balloons, ask for details and prices.

directions: Use paper and an envelope. Enclose a stamped addressed envelope.

ask for: 5 free printed balloon samples

write to: The Kite and Balloon Company
Old Church
160 Eardley Road
London SW16 5TG

the railway game

You have three stations to visit; they may be Dublin, Folkestone and Harrogate, but which is the quickest route to take? Send for this huge, full-colour Railway Game poster and learn more about British Rail's vast InterCity network of lines and stations as you race round the country trying to finish first. It's a game for six to eight players so you and your friends can have hours of fun trying to outsmart each other to see who can end their journey first. You may be hindered by a cow on the line or perhaps you have boarded the wrong train, but even if you finish last you'll have gained a lot of knowledge about Britain's major towns and cities and how to get to them by train. There are lots of fact sheets that would be very helpful if you were set a project on transport or the railways.

directions: Use a postcard

ask for: Railway Game
British Rail fact sheets

write to: British Rail Education Service
Euston House, 24 Eversholt Street
London NW1 1DZ

let's make it

These three packs from Help the Aged have lots of ideas for things to do in your spare time. The Recipe one has instructions for delicious home-made lemonade, gingerbread and many more including the mysterious Fridge Squidge. In the Craft Pack there are instructions for making all sorts of things from brooches. and badges to bird tables while the Fund Raising Pack has ideas for carol singing, jumble sales and toy fairs to raise money for charity. Send off for them now and banish boredom!

directions: Use paper and an envelope. Enclose a stamped addressed envelope (see below).

ask for: Fund Raising Pack (self-addressed envelope stamped with 14p)
Recipe Pack (self-addressed envelope stamped with 14p)
Craft Pack (self-addressed envelope stamped with 26p)
Fund Raising, Recipe & Craft Packs (self-addressed envelope stamped with 32p)

write to: Help the Aged C.F.R.
St James's Walk
London EC1R 0BE

a magic scratch

You don't have to be a good artist to get a perfect picture every time with this scratchboard kit. All you have to do is carefully scratch away the grey areas with the engraving tool to reveal the picture underneath. By varying the angle of the tool you can produce thick or thin strokes. Straight lines can be engraved using the edge of a steel rule as a guide but if you do make a mistake and scratch away the wrong part you can paint over it with Indian ink.

There is a wide range of subjects available including birds, animals and flowers. If you send for this sample Glo-art pack you will receive one copper-coloured picture and one multi-coloured one. Each kit comes complete with scraping tool.

directions: Use paper and an envelope. Enclose cheque or postal order for £1.25 and your address.

ask for: FSFK sample scratch-glo-art kit

write to: Hi-toys Ltd
Tresham Street
Kettering
Northants NN16 8SB

flicker stickers

How *do* these flicker stickers work? When moved to a slightly different angle, the picture you are looking at disappears only to be replaced by a different one. Stick them in scrapbooks, pencil cases, even on bedroom furniture, if you're allowed – the possibilities are endless.

directions: Use paper and an envelope. Enclose a postal order or cheque for £1.20 (*not* coins)

ask for: Flicker stickers

write to: Curious Caterpillar (FK)
73 Lancaster Rd
Hitchin, Herts SG5 1PE

clip-on charmers

These clip-ons are irresistible. Hang them on your curtains, or let them cling to your lapel or schoolbag, then they'll be with you all day long. Their heads swivel, so they can look in any direction; the only problem is – which one to choose? Select from Lion, Sheep, Bee, Cow, Puppy, Dinosaur.

directions: Use paper and an envelope. Enclose postal order or cheque for £1.30 (*not* coins)

ask for: Lion, Sheep, Bee, Cow, Puppy OR
Dinosaur clip-on

write to: Curious Caterpillar (FK)
73 Lancaster Rd
Hitchin, Herts SG5 1PE

pretty polly

How would you like a multi-coloured parrot living in your bedroom? No, this one doesn't make a noise and doesn't need feeding because it's a fun inflatable. Just blow it up and sit it on a shelf – it will make your friends look twice.

directions: Use paper and an envelope. Enclose £1.35 postal order or cheque (*not* coins).

ask for: Inflatable Parrot

write to: Curious Caterpillar (FK)
73 Lancaster Rd
Hitchin, Herts SG5 1PE

pot luck bag

When you send for this bag of toys from Curious Caterpillar you can't be quite sure what you're going to get. That's why it's called a pot luck bag. But there will be at least seven little toys inside assorted for boys and girls.

directions: Use paper and an envelope. Enclose a postal order or cheque for £1.50 (*not* coins)

ask for: Pot Luck Bag

write to: Curious Caterpillar (FK)
73 Lancaster Rd
Hitchin, Herts SG5 1PE

pastry cut-outs

Do you like making pastry and biscuits? Even if you haven't tried it, it's great fun – and you can enjoy a delicious treat after all your hard work. If you have friends for tea, it's also nice to be able to give them some fancy biscuits and pastries, and with this little set of four pastry cut-outs you'll be able to make biscuits like a professional cook.

directions: Use paper and an envelope. Please enclose £1.95.

ask for: Bird, Butterfly, Cat and Pig cutters

write to: David Mellor (FSFK)
4 Sloane Square
London SW1W 8EE

just a joke

Write to the Joke Shop by Post and they will send you a free gift and a catalogue which describes lots of other tricks and jokes. Then you can try them out on your friends ... or enemies!
There are lots of pop and football bargains, too.

directions: Use paper and an envelope. Enclose a 2nd class stamp plus your name and address.

ask for: Catalogue and free gift

write to: Joke Shop by Post (Dept FSK)
167 Winchester Road
Bristol BS4 3NJ

super stand-ups

These cheerful Salvation Army stand-ups come free of charge and will give you hours of fun. As you colour them in and cut them out you can find out more about the good work the Salvation Army does. For instance, there's Claire and Jenny with their mobile clinic, William and Paul with the tractor they use to teach villagers in poorer countries how to farm their land in the best way, Captain John preparing soup, and enough musicians to form a whole band.

You've probably heard the Salvation Army band playing in shopping centres, particularly around Christmas time. This is just one of the many things they do in the community, helping people both here in Britain and in many other countries around the world.

directions: Use a postcard

ask for: Salvation Army Stand-ups

write to: Schools' Information Service
The Salvation Army
101 Queen Victoria Street
London EC4P 4EP

colour me in

You will find out how people live in other countries with these lovely little colouring books. There are four titles: Dwellings, Transport, Crafts and Musical Instruments.

directions: Use paper and an envelope. Enclose 50p for each title you want (postage is free) plus a 9″ x 6¼″ self-addressed envelope.

ask for: Our World Colouring Book. You must state which title or titles you want.

write to: Dept FSFK
Shepheard-Walwyn Publishers
Suite 34, 26 Charing Cross Road
London WC2H 0DY

colour and send

How many times have you suddenly remembered it's someone's birthday and you can't get to the shops in time to buy a card? If you send for these colour and send cards, you'll always have one handy. There are six birthday cards and four 'get well' cards in each pack.

directions: Use paper and an envelope. Enclose postal order or cheque for £1.50.

ask for: pack of 10 colour and send cards

write to: The Comenius Company Ltd
17 Castle View Park
Mawnan Smith
Falmouth TR11 5HB

everlasting flowers

Now you can make your own attractive flower arrangement that will keep for years. With these two kits you can have either a Harvest Time arrangement of red poppies and blue cornflowers or a Woodland Arrangement of Rhododendrons and Blossoms in shades of violet and pink. You can also send for the Kaleidoscope booklet describing other kits available.

directions: Use paper and an envelope. Please enclose the correct money for the items you want plus 2 x 14p stamps with all requests.

ask for: Poppies & Cornflowers kit (£1)
Rhododendrons & Blossoms kit (£1)
Kaleidoscope of Tissue Paper Crafts(50p)
Free leaflet

write to: Yvonne Dockree Flowermaking Supplies
Field Cottage & Studio
Rodsley
Brailsford
Derbyshire DE6 3AL

fun with dyes

You can transform an old shirt, sweater or skirt with today's up-to-the-minute dyeing techniques. These free leaflets from Dylon have ideas on using their Color Fun range of paints and pens to provide some really stunning designs. You can use stencils, potato prints or free-hand drawing to give your clothes a new look.

The paints and pens are applied directly to the fabric. When your design is dry you can make it colour-fast by covering it with a clean, dry cloth and ironing on the painted area for just a minute or two. And did you know you can use your microwave for dyeing small articles? It's so easy – just 4 minutes on 'High' and you can produce stripy socks, tie-dye effects and many more unique patterns.

directions: Use paper and an envelope. Enclose a self-addressed stamped envelope.

ask for: Leaflets on:
Color Fun Fabric Paints and Pens
Color Fun Fabric Painting
Dylon Micro Dye

write to: Dylon International (FSFK)
Worsley Bridge Road
Lower Sydenham
London SW26 5HD

catalogue of crafts

Whether you're into beadcraft or raffiawork, this catalogue will help you with a current hobby or may start you off on a new one. It has details of materials for embroidery, tapestry, canework, marquetry, flower-making, jewellery and many more.

directions: Use paper and an envelope. Enclose 2 first class stamps.

ask for: Catalogue of handicraft materials

write to: Fred Aldous Ltd
The Handicraft Centre
PO Box 135
37 Lever Street, Manchester M60 1UX

make your own camera

Did you know that you can make a camera with a couple of pieces of cardboard, a piece of aluminium foil, black paper, masking tape, a sewing needle and a couple of rubber bands? And it actually works! Kodak will tell you how, and also send you details of other project ideas and photographic experiments.

directions: Use a postcard.

ask for: Kodak pinhole camera offer

write to: Kodak Limited
Publications Dept A11H
PO Box 66
Hemel Hempstead, Herts HP1 1JU

pins and peg dolls

Do you find you're always losing pins? This kit from Worthing Museum could solve all your problems. It contains a piece of felt, some coloured material, lace, ribbon, pins and beads and makes up into a charming Victorian pin holder in the shape of a hat. One of these would make a lovely gift for a special person.

The Museum will also send you a kit so that you can make Peggoty, this delightful little peg doll, in the traditional manner. All the materials you need are supplied and the instructions are written in a very clear, easy-to-understand way.

directions: Use paper and an envelope. Enclose a cheque for the correct amount (see below). Please do not enclose any postage stamps in payment or part-payment.

ask for: Pin holder hat (£1.10)
Peggoty (£1.30)

write to: Worthing Museum
Chapel Road
Worthing BN11 1HD

make a name for yourself

How would you like to make a very personal necklace for yourself? These kits from Janet Coles Beads come with letter beads to spell your name and over 100 tiny beads in many different colours – just say the name you want.

Any boys reading this might like to make a necklace up as a present for Mother's Day or as a gift for a sister or friend. Badges also make popular presents and these are great fun. All you have to do is glue the clasp on to the badge of your choice, using a fairly strong adhesive. The badges are made of wood and are brightly painted. Choose from teddy bear, orange cat or train.

directions: Use paper and an envelope. Enclose £1.25 for a glass bead name necklace with up to 7 letters or £1.55 for over 7 letters IN COINS ONLY, sellotaped firmly to your letter, PLUS two 14p stamps.
Send £2.00 IN COINS for a badge.

ask for: Glass bead name necklace (don't forget to say the name you want)
Teddy bear badge
Orange cat badge
Train badge

write to: Janet Coles Beads Ltd
Perdiswell Cottage
Bilford Road
Worcester WR3 8QA

historical connections

Who'd have thought that Guy Fawkes was a teenager when the Armada was defeated and you've no idea what the Elizabethan cure for epilepsy was! Find out by sending for this bookmark with more fascinating facts printed on it. There are also 5 historical broadsheets to choose from.

directions: Use paper and an envelope. Enclose a 9" x 4" stamped address envelope for bookmark or 50p plus a 1st class stamp if you want a broadsheet as well.

ask for: Historical Connections bookmark
Broadsheet on Romans, Vikings, Normans, Henry VIII or Queen Victoria.

write to: Historical Connections, 187a High Street Cranfield, Beds MK43 0JB

Ironbridge

The Ironbridge Gorge Museum takes its name from the world's first cast-iron bridge built across the River Severn near Telford. The Museum is on several sites and one 'passport' ticket will take you round all of them. Write for free leaflets about the Museum and a badge.

directions: Use paper and an envelope. Enclose a stamped self-addressed envelope.

ask for: Free Museum leaflets and badge

write to: Dept FSFK, Ironbridge Gorge Museum Ironbridge, Telford, Shropshire TF8 7AW

models in miniature

How would you like to own a cathedral just 1½ inches long? It's an exact replica of Canterbury Cathedral which is hundreds of years old. You can see what it looks like if you send for the ruler which has nine different scenes on it. There are lots of other things you can buy from the Cathedral Gift Shop and the sale of these souvenirs helps to keep this beautiful building in good repair.

directions: Use paper and an envelope. Enclose the money for the goods you want (see below) PLUS a first class stamp.

ask for: Miniature Cathedral model 1½″ long (£1.95)
Cathedral leather bookmark (80p)
   (red, blue or black)
Canterbury Cathedral woven badge (75p)
Look at Canterbury Cathedral (60p)
Cardboard cut-out model of Black Prince
   (60p)
Canterbury Cathedral 12″ ruler (55p)
Stained Glass tracing sheet (50p)
   (Nativity, Wars of the Roses, Crusaders
   or Noah's Ark)
Cathedral rubber (35p)

write to: Cathedral Gifts Ltd
3 The Precincts
Canterbury, Kent CT1 2EE

puzzle postcard

This little puzzle postcard from the National Army Museum could drive you mad! You have to get five balls into five holes. Sounds easy? But can you get the red ball to sit in the red hole and the blue ball in the blue hole and so on? For just 65p you can be amused for hours.

directions: Use paper and an envelope. Enclose 65p postal order or cheque.

ask for: 'Blister' puzzle postcard

write to: Museum Shop
National Army Museum
Royal Hospital Road, London SW3 4HT

on the right lines

Since it opened in 1975, the National Railway Museum has attracted well over 13 million visitors. Now you can obtain a 32-page full-colour Guide to the Museum, illustrating many of the massive exhibits, three postcards and one FREE Postcard.

directions: Use paper and an envelope. Enclose £2.00 and a self-addressed label.

ask for: The N.R.M. colour guide, 3 postcards and one FREE postcard.

write to: National Railway Museum
Dept FSFK
Leeman Rd, York YO2 4XJ

life among the pyramids

When you're given a project to do at school it isn't always easy to find the right illustration. These postcards from the Petrie Museum will make any topic on Ancient Egypt even more interesting. There are six in a set and include vases, carvings and paintings as well as the earliest linen dress that is nearly 5,000 years old.

The museum has also produced a 'Children's Trail' which, although designed to be used within the museum itself, has many facts about Ancient Egypt as well as pictures to colour. Then the next time you're in London you could visit the Petrie Museum taking your 'Children's Trail' booklet with you.

directions: Use paper and an envelope. Enclose the correct money for the items you want.

ask for: Set of six postcards of Ancient Egyptian artefacts (£1.00)
Petrie Museum Children's Trail (50p)

write to: Petrie Museum
Department of Egyptology
University College
Gower Street
London WC1E 6BT

digging for history

Only archaeologists know the excitement of discovering our lost history by digging below the surface of our towns, villages and countryside. You can share in the fun by keeping up with news of recent digs in the magazine of the Young Archaeologists Club. It's packed with lots of other information, offers and competitions. There are also details of how to join the Club.

directions: Use paper and an envelope. Enclose a postal order for 70p and a 22p s.a.e.

ask for: A copy of Young Archaeology.

write to: Dominic Tinner
Young Archaeologists Club
37 Micklegate
York YO1 1JH

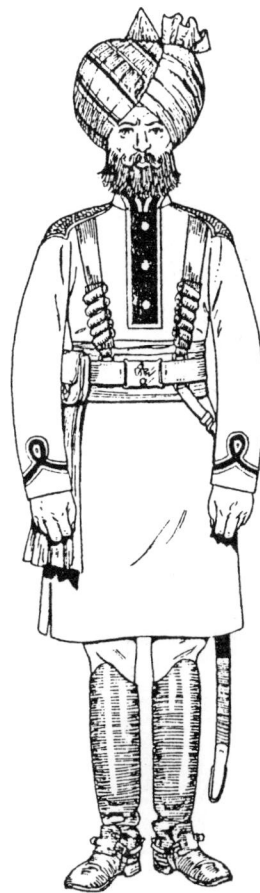

uniformly correct!

If your interest is in historic army uniforms then these colouring sheets will fit the bill. Colouring details are given on each sheet so that you can have an accurate record of how these nineteenth century soldiers really looked.

directions: Use paper and an envelope. Enclose 65p.

ask for: 5 Army Uniform colouring sheets.

write to: Museum Shop, National Army Museum
Royal Hospital Road
London SW3 4HT

what shall I wear?

Sarah-Ann is a doll of the 1880's. Her cut-out clothes slip over her head and have a back as well as a front. She has a party dress, silk dress with bustle, cami-knickers and corsets, flannel underwear for winter and much more. You can play with her for hours.

directions: Use paper and an envelope. Enclose 50p plus 48p in stamps.

ask for: Sarah-Ann cut-out doll

write to: Publications Dept.
York Castle Museum
York YO1 1RY

fancy bazaar

You'll have great fun making up this Victorian shop which is very similar to many on display in York Castle Museum. There are figures to cut out too and a horse and carriage so you'll have a complete Victorian street scene to build up.

directions: Use paper and an envelope. Enclose 50p plus 48p in stamps.

ask for: Fancy bazaar cut-out

write to: Publications Dept.
York Castle Museum
York YO1 1RY

Bath through the ages

If you enjoy model making and are also interested in history, then this ingenious 3-D cut-out model of the Marquess of Lansdowne is just for you. It requires patience and careful handling to put it together, but the finished article will look really splendid.

Bath Museum is also offering a set of three 19th century cut-out and colour dolls, a book called *Bath from Roman Times* and an unusual press-out 'tin' mask (made of cardboard) which is a copy of a Roman one dug up in the temple of Sulis Minerva. Your teacher would be interested to see these things, too.

directions: Use paper and an envelope. Enclose postal order or cheque for the correct amount (see below).

ask for: Marquess of Lansdowne cut-out 50p + p&p
Set of three 19th century cut-out dolls 75p + p&p
Press-out Roman 'tin' mask 25p + p&p
Bath from Roman Times £1.50 + p&p
(Postage is 35p for one item or 50p if 2 or more are ordered)

write to: Mementos of Bath
Pump Room
Stall Street
Bath, Avon

BEND BACK ALONG THIS LINE

toys of yesterday

Most children in the early years of this century had just a few favourite toys that they played with over and over again. That is why toys in museums sometimes look a little shabby, but it is only because they were loved and used, often being passed on to younger brothers and sisters and then to their own children.

One of the most popular toys was the Noah's Ark because the collection of animals that went in the ark could get bigger and bigger. One of the largest arks had over 400 animals. This colouring book from the Museum of Childhood has illustrations of many toys that your parents, grandparents and even great-grandparents might have played with.

Other things you can send off for are a wooden yoyo, badge, pencil, eraser and a story telling what happened when all the museum's toys came alive.

directions: Use paper and an envelope. Enclose a stamped addressed envelope for the free postcard list or the correct money for the item you want, as shown below.

ask for: Museum of Childhood Colouring book (£1.50)

Badge (50p)   Eraser (50p)
Pencil (50p)   Wooden Yoyo (£1.00)

Royal Mile at Midnight storybook (£2.00)
Free postcard list

write to: Free Stuff for Kids
Huntly House Museum
142 Canongate
Edinburgh EH8 8DD

Roman life

Why not give your room a Roman look with these replicas from Corinium Museum? Craftsmen in those days made wonderful mosaics and you can buy six different colouring sheets showing some of the designs used. You can also send for a wooden ruler, 40cms long, showing both modern and Roman measurements, a pack of reproduction Roman coins, a gold twisted torc for your wrist and an unusual Roman coin choker that would make a different present for someone special.

directions: Use paper and an envelope. Enclose cheque or postal order for 95p for *each* mosaic sheet, £1.35 for the Roman ruler, £1.20 per pack of 4 coins, £2.15 for the Roman Coin Choker and £1.20 for the torc. (All prices include postage and packing.)

ask for: Mosaic colouring sheet of:
Hare, Peacock, Battling Gladiators, Peltae Design, Rudston Charioteer, Sea God.
Roman ruler (wooden)
Roman coin pack
Roman coin choker
Gold twisted torc

write to: Corinium Museum
Park Street, Cirencester
Gloucestershire GL7 2BX

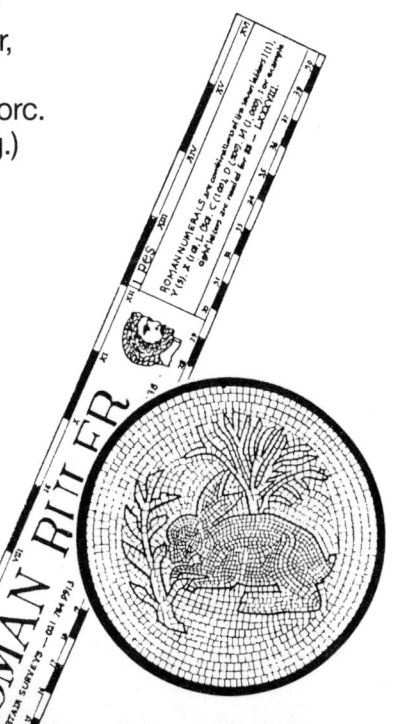

the gold of the pharaohs

The pharaohs, or kings, of Ancient Egypt were very wealthy people and when they died they had many of their most precious possessions buried with them. This is why we know so much about them today. Although some of the tombs were plundered by robbers hundreds of years ago, other tombs remained untouched until they were excavated by archaeologists earlier this century.

The City of Edinburgh recently held an exhibition called 'The Gold of the Pharaohs' and published a full-colour wallchart, postcards and a little story book to accompany the exhibition. The wallchart has a brief history of the royal city of Tanis where all the treasures shown on the chart were found, and the postcards show some of these discoveries in greater detail. The story is called *The Pharaoh's Gold Mask* and tells of a young boy's first experiences of school about 3,000 years ago and how his craftsman father was asked to make a gold mask for the pharaoh.

directions: Use paper and an envelope. Send postal order or cheque *only* (not coins or stamps) for the correct money. All prices include postage and packing.

ask for: Treasures of Tanis wallchart (£2.00)
Set of 6 coloured postcards of the
　　Treasures of Tanis (£1.50)
The Pharaoh's Gold Mask story (£1.50)

write to: Free Stuff for Kids
Huntly House Museum
142 Canongate
Edinburgh EH8 8DD

activity history

Shopping for an Anglo-Saxon king can't have been much fun. At one feast, given by the King of Wessex, the guests ate their way through 10 jars of honey, 300 loaves, 42 casks of ale, 12 oxen, 10 geese, 20 hens, 10 cheeses, a cask of butter and 5 salmon. How much do you know about the Anglo-Saxons? This activity book has lots of facts about the way they lived and worked, the clothes and jewellery they wore as well as puzzles, quizzes and things to colour.

There are six activity books in the series and you can also send for a booklet about the British Museum and another on the Museum of Mankind.

directions: Use paper and an envelope. Enclose the correct money (postal order or cheque) for each book you want PLUS 55p p&p for 1 item or £1.10 p&p for 2 or more.

ask for: The Anglo-Saxons Activity Book (£1.95)
The Ancient Egyptians Activity Book (£1.95)
The Ancient Greeks Activity Book (£1.95)
The Romans Activity Book (£1.95)
The Vikings Activity Book (£1.95)
The Celts Activity Book (£1.95)
Inside the British Museum (£1.95)
From Aztecs to Zulus: Inside the Museum of Mankind (£1.95)

write to: Book Promotions Manager (FSFK)
British Museum Publications
46 Bloomsbury Street
London WC1B 3QQ

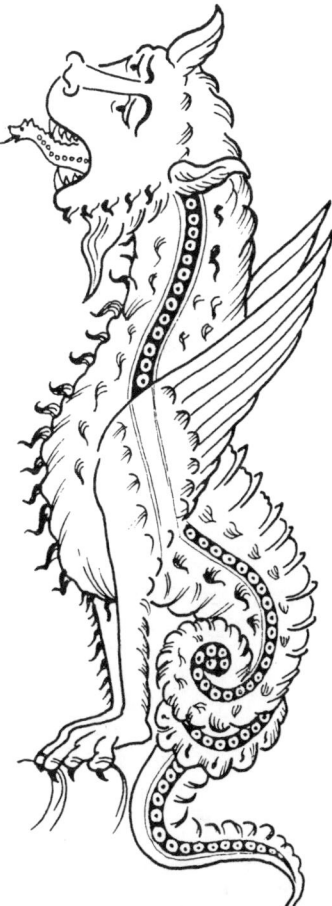

construct a cathedral

This is the easy way to build your own cathedral. Instead of bricks and cement all you need are scissors and glue. Colour the model in first and then, if you follow the instructions, you will have your very own miniature cathedral. The real Durham Cathedral is a magnificent Norman building which stands on a hill towering over the town and the River Wear.

As well as the cut-out model, you can also send for a ruler showing nine different views of the Cathedral and a rubber with an illustration of the Cathedral on it.

directions: Use paper and an envelope. Enclose the correct money (see below).

ask for: Durham Cathedral Model £1.50 plus 30p postage
Durham Cathedral Ruler 70p plus 20p postage
Durham Cathedral Rubber 45p plus 20p postage

write to: The Cathedral Bookshop
S.P.C.K.
Durham Cathedral
Durham DH1 3EQ

museum of surprises

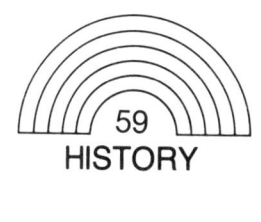

The Castle Museum in York has many surprises inside including streets of little shops set out just as they used to be many years ago. You can make up a model of one of these streets from a kit that the Museum will send you. They also have a packet of scraps with boys· and girls dressed in the fashions of the last century and tiny little Nursery Rhyme Chapbooks reprinted from 19th century originals. Six titles are available.

directions: Use paper and an envelope. Send your name and address and the correct money for the items you want PLUS 25% (¼) of the total sales price to cover postage and packing (minimum charge for p. & p. is 25p up to a maximum £2.50)

ask for: Scraps 40p + 20p p.&p.
Street model 75p + 20p p.&p.
Nursery Rhyme Books: Simple Simon, Old Mother Hubbard, Jack Sprat, Cock Robin, Tommy Tucker, Dame Trot 25p each + 20p p.&p.

write to: Publications Dept
York Castle Museum
York YO1 1RY

building Stonehenge

If you've ever visited Stonehenge or seen pictures of it you've probably wondered how those huge stones were put there 5,000 years ago. This colouring book tells you how archaeologists think it was done.

directions: Use paper and an envelope. Enclose 80p postal order or cheque.

ask for: The Early Man and Stonehenge colouring book (80p inc p&p)

write to: Salisbury Museum Replicas (FSFK)
The Kings House, 65 The Close
Salisbury, Wilts SP1 2EN

the colourful canals

The canals of Britain were once busy with brightly painted barges carrying goods up and down the country. The barge people decorated their pots and pans, too, with bold flower designs and other patterns. You can learn more about the history of the canals in the Waterways Museum at Stoke Bruerne. This colouring card from there will give you just a taste of canal life.

directions: Use paper and an envelope. Send 50p coin sellotaped firmly to your letter.

ask for: The Waterways Museum colouring card

write to: The Waterways Museum
Stoke Bruerne, Towcester
Northants NN12 7SE

crossword crazy

Do you enjoy doing crosswords? If so, you'll love these historical ones. They are poster size so you can stick them on your bedroom wall and fill in a few clues at a time. They have a hundred or more clues each and you may have to search in your history books or encyclopaedias for some of the answers, but it's great fun and you'll be learning a lot more about different historical periods at the same time.

The crosswords available are listed below and there are also colour-in posters of the same period that would pair nicely with the crossword ones.

directions: Use paper and an envelope. Enclose 75p postal order or cheque for any one poster or £1.40 for two. (Prices include postage and packing.)

ask for: Crossword poster and/or a colour-in poster of: Egyptian life; Roman life; Anglo-Saxons; Vikings; Normans; Medieval times; Tudor times; Early Stuarts; Georgian times; Victorian times; the Edwardians.

write to: The Comenius Company Ltd
17 Castle View Park
Mawnan Smith
Falmouth
Cornwall TR11 5HB

dangle a dongle

A dongle is a vertical wooden jigsaw puzzle designed to hang on the wall. It comes with your own initials or name cut out of it. And you can choose whether you have a bird, cat, palm tree, umbrella, teddy bear, Christmas tree or flower motif at the bottom.

directions:	Use paper and an envelope. Enclose 80p for each letter of your name or initial.
ask for:	A dongle. State the initials and motif that you want.
write to:	Dept FSFK, Puzzleplex Stubbs Walden, Doncaster DN6 9BY

1066 and all that

The Bayeux Tapestry is not only an incredible piece of craftsmanship, but it is also a record of the Battle of Hastings and you can send for two colouring sheets of part of it. There are also colouring sheets of life in the Roman town of Silchester.

directions:	Use paper and an envelope. Enclose 20p for each colouring sheet and 15p for p&p
ask for:	Bayeux Tapestry colouring sheets: 'Preparing for the Invasion' 'The Battle' Roman Silchester colouring sheets: 'Carpenter's Workshop' 'Kitchen'
write to:	Museum and Art Gallery Blagrave Street, Reading RG1 1QH

raise a smile

Do you need locking up? This badge says you do. Wear it and watch passers-by smile. There's another one that advises you to 'Wind down on the canals' and a little furry creature saying 'I've got the Waterways Bug'. They are all available from British Waterways who also have two splendid woven badges, a key ring and bookmarks all reminding us of the many miles of canals and inland waterways that we have in Britain.

directions: Use paper and an envelope. Enclose the correct money (see below) plus 40p postage and packing for up to 4 items ordered or 80p for 5 or more items ordered. Send postal order or cheque only, *not* stamps.

ask for: Canals of Britain Bookmark 25p
Leather key ring – Britain's Inland
   Waterways 95p
Fuzz Bug 45p
Slogan badge (either 'I need locking up' or
   'Wind down on the Canals') 65p
Sew-on badge: Britain's Inland Waterways
   £1.25
'Inland Waterways' sticky badge 85p

write to: Canal Shop & Mail Order Dept (FSFK)
British Waterways, Melbury House
Melbury Terrace, London NW1 6JX

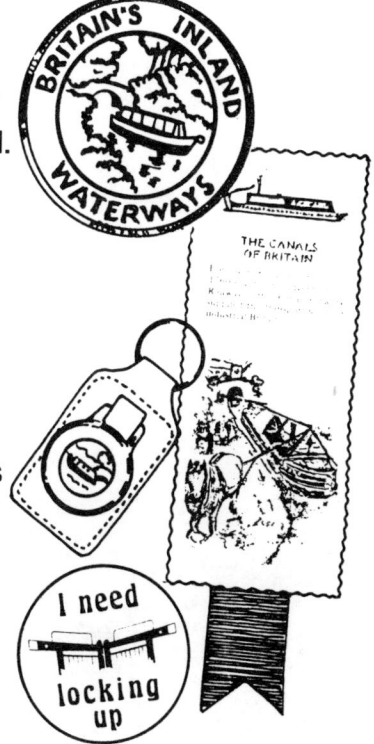

a spoonful of ...

Eating your breakfast grapefruit will be easy with these special spoons from Outspan, who will send you free booklets, a poster and citrus peeler as well.

directions: Use paper and an envelope. Enclose 70p and s.a.e. if you would like the grapefruit spoons as well as the other things listed.

ask for: 4 grapefruit spoons (70p); Citrus peeler (free); Poster (free); The Story of Outspan (free); The Food Value of Citrus (free); Learning to Swim with Oscar Outspan (free)

write to: Juliet Barton
Advertising Dept. Outspan Organisation
PO Box 137, Berkhamsted HP4 1AN

this takes the biscuit

Here is an unusual model of a Huntley & Palmer biscuit tin in the shape of one of their delivery vans. This cut-out model from Reading Museum comes complete with full instructions.

directions: Use paper and an envelope. Enclose 45p.

ask for: Cut-out model of Huntley & Palmer delivery van

write to: Museum and Art Gallery
Blagrave Street
Reading,
Berkshire RG1 1QH

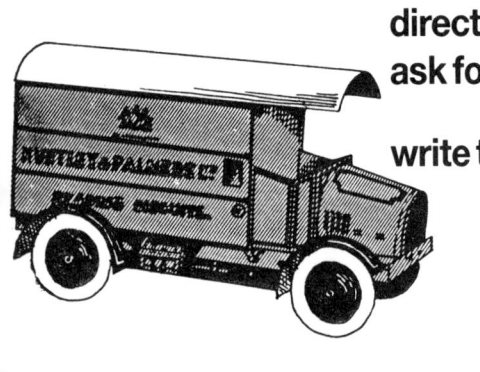

a right to be left

If you are left-handed, this special pair of left-handed scissors will take all the hard work out of cutting paper. You can also send for a Lefthanders Badge and a catalogue.

directions: Use paper and an envelope. Enclose £2.00 plus 35p p&p for Lefty Scissors, 40p plus 15p p&p for a badge, three 14p stamps for catalogue only.

ask for: Lefty paper scissors; Lefthanders Badge 'I've a right to be left'; catalogue.

write to: Anything Left-handed Ltd
65 Beak Street, London W1R 3LF

understanding the bible

Do you find the Bible difficult to read and understand?: Many people do, and not just children either. But help is at hand. The Scripture Union has produced two booklets to help you find your way around the Bible. There is *Quest* for the under tens and *One to One* for elevens and over.

directions: Use paper and an envelope. Enclose 50p. If you send a coin, sellotape it to your letter.

ask for: Either: *Quest* (for under tens) OR *One to One* (for elevens and over)

write to: Quest Special Offer
(OR One to One Special Offer)
Scripture Union
130 City Road, London EC1V 2NJ

HAVE YOU ENCLOSED THE CORRECT MONEY?

name it – it's yours

Have you noticed how pencils and pens have a habit of getting lost, keys hide under newspapers and wellies wander off? *Toys and Things* have come up with some good ideas to stamp out these annoying habits. You can order pencil blocks, key rings and welly pegs which have your name burnt into the wood, then everything can be kept in its proper place. The key rings come in five different shapes: round, oval, oblong, triangle and heart. Just say which shape and name you want. *Toys and Things* also do wooden egg cups and small wooden spoons.

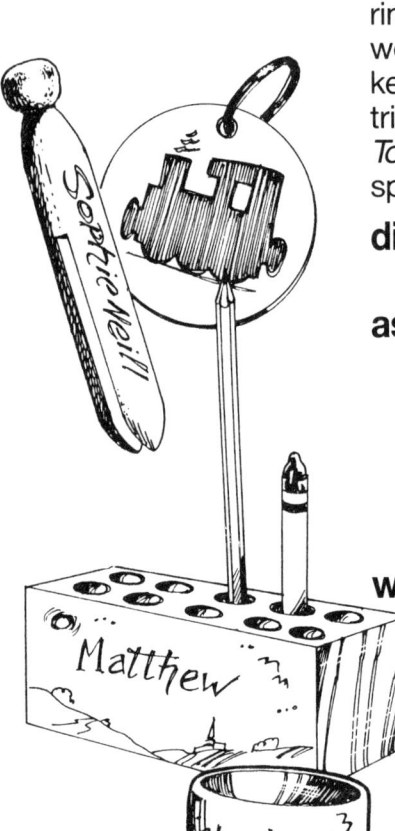

directions: Use paper and an envelope. Send <u>postal order</u> or <u>cheque</u> for the correct amount.

ask for: Pencil block £1.90 + 30p p&p
Key ring 90p (+ 25p p&p for up to 4 key rings)
Welly pegs 25p (+ 25p p&p for up to 7 pegs)
Egg Cup 90p + 30p p&p
Wooden spoon 80p + 30p p&p

write to: Toys and Things
10 Long Croft
Aston-on-Trent
Derby DE7 2UH

pin on a pig

Or a rabbit or an elephant. Yes, you can do just that with these delightful metal badges from *Toys and Things*. There are ten different ones to choose from. Buy one for yourself or as a present for a friend. The badges available are: horse, cat, pig, rabbit, elephant, hand, moon, star, toadstool and owl. Why not buy your bedroom door a badge too? Well it's a plaque, really, but it could stop brothers and sisters from coming in uninvited. It could say: 'Please knock' or 'Mark's room' or 'Susan's study' or perhaps 'The Pig Sty' would be more appropriate! If you share a room there are double plaques with enough space for two names on them.

directions: Use paper and an envelope. Enclose <u>postal order</u> or <u>cheque</u> for the correct amount (see below).

ask for: Boxed metal badge of: horse, cat, pig, rabbit, elephant, hand, moon, star, toadstool or owl. (State which one you want.) £1.00 each (+ 25p p&p for up to 4 badges)

Leather badge (flower design) 80p each + 25p p&p for up to 15 badges

Door plaques (with sticky pads) 80p each + 25p p&p

Round double door plaques (with 2 names) £1.30 + 25p p&p

(Don't forget to state the names or words you want)

write to: Toys & Things, 10 Long Croft Aston-on-Trent, Derby DE7 2UH

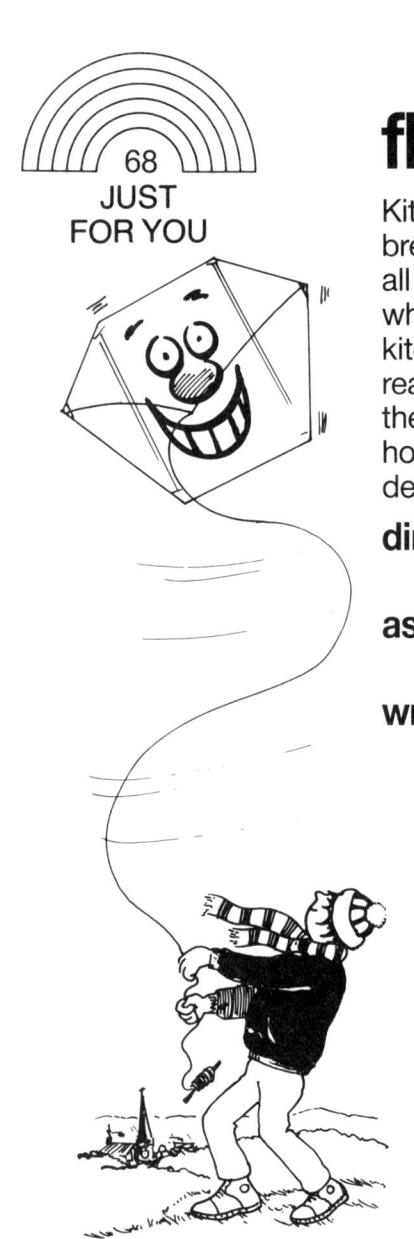

fly your kite

Kite flying is enormous fun for people of all ages. A warm breezy day brings them out into fields and parks with kites of all sizes, shapes and colours. If you've never tried kite flying, why not send off for these free instructions for making a sled kite which has been specially designed for FREE STUFF readers by the Kite and Balloon Company of London. Most of the materials for it will probably already be lying around your house just waiting to made up into a kite. Then you can decorate it in any way you choose to make it really unique.

directions: Use paper and an envelope. Enclose
a stamped addressed envelope.

ask for: Instruction sheet on how to make
a sled kite

write to: The Kite and Balloon Company
Old Church
160 Eardley Road
London SW16 5TG

eggs-citing facts!

Did you know that, not only are eggs good to eat, but if rubbed into your hair they will make it shiny and if mixed with honey and witch hazel they make an effective anti-sunburn cream? These and other fascinating and useful facts are included in the leaflet *Take a new look at eggs.* You can help to make some of the exotic dishes included in this leaflet, like Thai egg fried rice, egg and coconut curry or huevos rancheros (Mexican fried eggs, to you!)

directions: Use paper and an envelope. Enclose an A4 size stamped addressed envelope.

ask for: *Egg Facts* fact sheet
Leaflets:
Eating for a healthy life
Take a new look at eggs

write to: Free Stuff for Kids
British Egg Information Service
126-128 Cromwell Road
London SW7 4ET

the all-round cheese

Have you ever wondered how cheese is transformed from milk, straight from the cow, into that delicious yellow wedge sitting on your plate? The Dutch Dairy Bureau have produced a large full-colour poster which explains it all.

We are all familiar with the red round shape of Edam cheese, but did you know how good it is cooked? By combining it with meat, fish or vegetables you can produce a whole week's menu of different taste experiences. These recipe leaflets from the Dutch Dairy Bureau have easy instructions for dishes like Edam seafood stir-fry, chicken breasts gourmet, vegetarian gratin and a delicious cheesy apple flan. Write to the Bureau now and give the family a treat.

directions: Use paper and an envelope. Enclose a 24p stamp.

ask for: How the Dutch make yellow cheese from white milk
Recipe leaflets

write to: The Dutch Dairy Bureau (FSFK offer)
4 Swan Court
Leatherhead
Surrey KT22 8AH

packed lunches

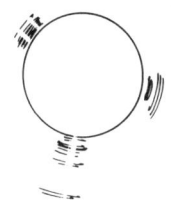

This leaflet contains delicious recipes as well as hints and tips to make any packed lunch interesting and nutritious. The *Vegetarian Cooking* leaflet contains a variety of recipes for those wishing either to eat less meat or to follow a vegetarian diet.

Recipes from Around the World is a colourful leaflet containing savoury and sweet recipes from many different countries. For that special occasion there's a leaflet on iced desserts with mouth-watering dishes like Biscuit Tortoni and Cassata.

directions: Use paper and an envelope. Enclose a stamped addressed envelope 12″ x 10″.

ask for: Packed Lunches leaflet
Vegetarian Cooking leaflet
Recipes from Around the World leaflet
Iced Desserts leaflet

write to: The Kraft Kitchen (FSFK Offer),
Kraft Foods Ltd.,
St. George's House,
Bayshill Road,
Cheltenham,
Gloucestershire
GL50 3AE

pure natural butter

How much do you know about butter? Find out all there is to know – from the cow to the table. If you're between the ages of 6 and 11 you'll find lots of facts about butter, plus things to do, in the leaflet *All About Butter.* There are recipes for pizza and gingerbread men, instructions on how to make butter using just cream, a screw top jar and a fork, and a page full of word games and puzzles.

However, if you're older than 11 the Butter Information Council will send you a project pack entitled *Nature's Miracle – the Story of Butter.* This is simply bursting with facts; it includes information on growing grass, the dairy cow, dairy farm buildings and machinery, right through to the history of butter and the structure and characteristics of dietary fats.

directions: Use a postcard and write your age on it.

ask for: *All about Butter* leaflet OR
Nature's Miracle project pack

write to: Butter Information Council Ltd., Dept FSK
Tubs Hill House
London Road
Sevenoaks
Kent TN13 1BL

the story of coffee

King Charles II tried to ban coffee when it was first introduced into Britain, but there was such an outcry that within 10 days the new coffee shops that were springing up all over London were open for business again. Nestlé will send you a free 50-page Ladybird book on coffee, plus information sheets which tell you the whole story.

directions: Use a postcard

ask for: The Nestlé Coffee Kit

write to: The Nestlé Company Ltd. (Education Dept)
St George's House
Croydon, Surrey CR9 1NR

find out about tea

Because we drink tea every day, we don't think about it very much. Find out more about the story of tea from leaf to pot. Learn about the tea smugglers who used to hide tea chests in secret passages and about the sailing clippers which were used for transporting tea.

directions: Use paper and an envelope. Please enclose 2 first class stamps.

ask for: Tea Broadsheet

write to: The Tea Council Ltd. (FSK)
Sir John Lyon House
5 High Timber Street, London EC4V 3NJ

a taste of Germany

Is your town 'twinned' with a German one? Many British towns and villages are, so it's useful to know something about Germany when a party from your twin town comes to visit. The free full-colour booklet *Food and Drink from Germany* not only tells you about the food for which that country is famous, but also includes facts and figures about its agriculture and a brief account of its history, so is a good source of project material, too. There are also leaflets on the many different kinds of cheeses and sausages that are made in Germany as well as some mouth-watering ways of using them in cooked dishes.

directions: Use paper and an envelope. Enclose a self-addressed envelope 10½″ x 8½″.

ask for: Food and Drink from Germany
Leaflets on Cheeses and Sausages

write to: CMA UK Office
44-46 Knightsbridge
London SW1X 7JN

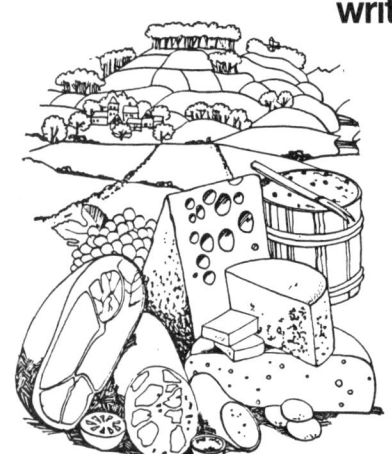

REMEMBER TO ADD YOUR NAME AND ADDRESS!

musical lives

We are used to hearing the music of great composers, but we often know very little about them. These attractive wall charts from Chimera have portraits of the composers as well as facts and illustrations connected with their lives.

directions: Use paper and an envelope. Enclose 90p *each* if ordering 1 or 2 charts OR 85p *each* if ordering 3 or more at the same time.

ask for: Bach, Bartok, Beethoven, Berlioz, Brahms, Britten, Debussy, Dvorak, Elgar, Handel, Haydn, Liszt, Mozart, Purcell, Schubert, Sibelius, Stravinsky, Tchaikovsky, Vaughan Williams, Verdi or Wagner wallchart.

write to: Chimera, 64 High Street
Cumnor, Oxford OX2 9QD

know the code

If we all knew and practised the Green Cross Code there'd be less accidents on the road. Get Mum and Dad to do it, too.

directions: Use a postcard. Remember to print clearly.

ask for: Green Cross Code material

write to: Information Division
Room S13/11
Department of Transport
2 Marsham Street
London SW1P 3EB

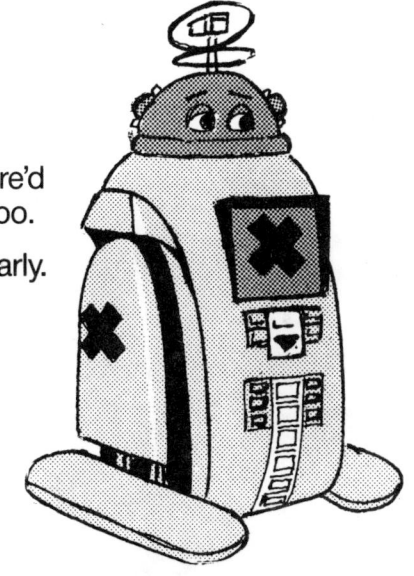

build your own cottage

Fiddler's Green is the name of the little village you can make with these attractive construction cards. There is a thatched cottage, a shepherd's cottage, a cartshed with a cart, and a grist mill. The only material you need are a pair of scissors, some glue and a pin to fix the sails on to the windmill. Not only can you have fun making your village but you can also learn about the buildings, what they were used for and how they were built. Did you know that some thatched roofs were made from heather? Or that they only need replacing about once in a lifetime? The grist mill dates from medieval times and there are still many to be seen in England. Look out for them the next time you are touring around the countryside.

directions: Use paper and an envelope. Enclose postal order or cheque for £1.00 (inc p&p)

ask for: Set of 4 postcard models:
Thatched cottage
Shepherd's cottage
Cartshed
Grist mill

write to: Cotswold Countryside Collection
Northleach
Cheltenham
Glos. GL54 3JH

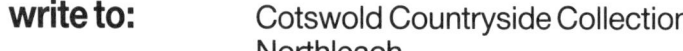

unearthing the past

It must be very exciting to dig up a brooch or piece of pottery that hasn't been seen for hundreds or even thousands of years. If you've ever thought of becoming an archaeologist, this publication will tell you more about it.

directions: Use paper and an envelope. Enclose a strong stamped addressed envelope 9" x 6½".

ask for: A copy of 'A Job in Archaeology'

write to: Council for British Archaeology
'A Job in Archaeology' offer
112 Kennington Road
London SE11 6RE

follow the country code

If you use this bookmark from the Countryside Commission you'll always be able to follow the Country Code. There's a large, black and white poster for you to colour and an access charter card that tells you about rights of way.

directions: Use paper and an envelope. Enclose a stamped addressed envelope 12" x 8½".

ask for: Country Code bookmark, poster and access charter card.

write to: Countryside Commission
Publications Despatch Department
19-23 Albert Road
Manchester M19 2EQ

read, colour and play

A game to play, a poster to colour and a crossword to do and you'll be learning your road safety drill at the same time.

directions: Use paper and an envelope. Enclose £1.95.

ask for: Road Safety Pack

write to: The Comenius Company Ltd.
17 Castle View Park, Mawnan Smith
Falmouth, Cornwall

I like books

Aunts, uncles and grandparents always ask what you'd like for your birthday and it is often difficult to decide. These leaflets give lists of books with brief descriptions of each plus the age group for which they are suitable. It could be the answer to your problem.

directions: Use paper and an envelope. Enclose a 9½" x 6½" stamped addressed envelope plus *10p stamp* or postal order (payable to F.C.B.G.) for *each* leaflet.

ask for: List of: 50 modern picture books;
50 recommended poetry books;
50 recommended books for teenagers;
50 best books for a birthday (all ages);
50 recommended books for children of
8-12; Pick of the year 1988

write to: Debbie Venables
23 Charlecote Drive, North Millers Dale
Chandlers Ford, Hampshire

Arthur One

For just 50p you can join the Arthur One Club. The mascot of the Ambulance Service, Arthur One gets very upset when one of his friends is hurt or injured. So remember – whatever you are doing, at school, at home or at play: *Think safe – be safe – stay safe* and make Arthur One happy.

You will receive a sticker, membership certificate and a newsletter twice a year.

directions: Use paper and an envelope. Give name, date of birth and enclose a stamped addressed envelope and 50p. If you enclose a coin, sellotape it firmly to your letter.

ask for: Arthur One Club membership

write to: Arthur One
Caxton Hall
88/92 Chapel Street
Salford
Manchester M3 7AY

BEE-BAA
AMBULANCE

be energy-wise

Do you know how to save energy in your home? Do you know about safety in the home? And do you know about Gas Safety? With this free leaflet from British Gas you will be able to find out more about these three important subjects. There is an *Energy House Snake and Ladders* game in which you have to add the snakes and ladders yourself by deciding, first of all, which pictures are energy-saving and which are energy-wasting. Then you can have fun playing it. There is also a *Be Safe at Home* picture quiz for you to do. When you have learned where all the hazards are, you can make your own Home Safety poster. The 'missing words' quiz' is also very useful as it shows both children and adults what to do in case of a gas leak.

Why not send for this free leaflet and make learning about gas fun?

directions: Use a postcard

ask for: The Energy House snakes and ladders game

write to: British Gas Education Service
PO Box 46
Hounslow
Middlesex TW4 6NF

a dinosaur called Claws

While fossil hunting in 1983 Mr William Walker found a clawbone of a flesh-eating dinosaur. You can read more about this amazing find in the colour booklet *Claws* from the Natural History Museum.

directions: Use paper and an envelope. Enclose postal order or cheque made payable to British Museum (Natural History)

ask for: Claws booklet 75p (inc p&p)
Set of 5 Claws postcards £1.25 (inc p&p)

write to: Sales Dept. (FSFK)
Natural History Museum Publications
Cromwell Road, London SW7 5BD

did you know ...

Beefeaters weren't called that because they liked eating meat? The name came from the French word boufitiers because they were the guardians of the King's food or buffet. Now, not many people know that! You can find out more about London's famous people and places with this London Capital colour and read poster. And if you enjoy doing crosswords you'll love tackling this giant one that has over 100 clues.

directions: Use paper and an envelope. Enclose £1.40

ask for: London Material Pack

write to: The Comenius Company Ltd
17 Castle View Park, Mawnan Smith
Falmouth, Cornwall TR11 5HB

canal life

Lots of people love canals with their boats, locks, and old barges. At one time most of Britain's trade went on these waterways, and at the height of the canal building boom there were over 6,000 miles of navigable rivers and canals. These items capture some of the magic of canals. There's a 1/76 cardboard scale model of the motor boat 'Ian', cardboard cut-outs of a canalboat cabin at the turn of this century, cut-outs of a canalboat horse and of a boatman and woman of the same period, a colouring-in book all about canals, and a Ladybird book on the history of the canals.

directions: Use paper and an envelope. Please enclose 40p postage for up to 4 items or 80p for more than 4 items, plus the amount (postal order or cheque, *not* stamps) for each item you want.

ask for: Cardboard cut-outs:
  Motor boat 'Ian' (£1.10)
  Canalboat cabin (£1.10)
  Canalboat horse (35p)
  Boatman and woman (35p)
Canal colouring book (35p)
The story of our Canals – Ladybird (99p)

write to: Canal Shop & Mail Order Dept (FSFK)
British Waterways
Melbury House
Melbury Terrace
London NW1 6JX

learn Esperanto

Esperanto is a language that has no difficult grammar. It was invented over a hundred years ago to make life easier when people of different countries wanted to talk to each other. Millions of people now learn it all over the world, and you can have a go yourself with 12 free lessons by post.

directions: Give your age. Use paper and an envelope. Enclose a 9″ x 4½″ s.a.e.

ask for: First lesson of the Twelve-part Free Postal Course in Esperanto

write to: Esperanto Centre
140 Holland Park Avenue
London W11 4UF

HM Coastguard

HM Coastguard is responsible for coordinating search and rescue operations around the 2,500 miles of Britain's coastline, and for 1,000 miles into the Atlantic. The Coastguard deals with many distress calls from swimmers in difficulty to collision at sea.

directions: Use a postcard. Remember to print your name and address clearly.

ask for: Leaflets and posters on the Coastguard Service

write to: Coastguard Publicity (S11/05)
Department of Transport
2 Marsham Street, London SW1P 3EO

a cheerful nag

This long colourful poster will help you to remember when to wash your hands, clean your teeth and have a bath – so Mum won't need to remind you any more!

directions: Use paper and an envelope. Please enclose an extra large stamped addressed envelope using either a 14p or 19p stamp.

ask for: Time to Wash

write to: British Bathroom Council
Federation House, Station Road
Stoke-on-Trent, Staffs ST4 2RT

be safe on water

If you are planning a holiday on or near water this year this publication will tell you how to enjoy the water safely.

directions: Use paper and an envelope. Enclose postal order or cheque for the correct amount.

ask for: Water Safety (Ladybird) 99p plus 40p (p&p)

write to: Information Centre (BWW)
British Waterways
Melbury House, Melbury Terrace
London NW1 6JX

HAVE YOU ENCLOSED THE CORRECT MONEY?

dinosaur fun

You sometimes see old films on TV where dinosaurs are chasing cavemen for a nice juicy supper. But that's only a story – the dinosaurs lived millions of years before man existed. These four posters from the Natural History Museum show you the dinosaurs in their natural setting and you can see just how big some of them were as they stand in a landscape of tall trees.

The Museum also has some splendid models of dinosaurs which are all on a 1/40th scale, so if you can imagine the real ones being 40 times bigger than the models you'll be glad they're not around now!

directions: Use paper and an envelope. Enclose cheque or postal order for the correct amount plus 50p p&p for each item ordered.

ask for: Poster (50p each) of:
Stegosaurus   Diplodocus
Triceratops   Tyrannosaurus rex
Model of:
Megalosaurus (75); Scelidosaurus (35p);
Triceratops (£1.00); Stegosaurus (75p);
Tyrannosaurus rex (£1.00);
Iguanodon (£1.00); Pteranodon (35p);
Plesiosaur (£1.00); Woolly mammoth (£1.00);
Blue Whale (£1.00); Ichthyosaur (£1.00).
(Don't forget to add postage.)

write to: Publication Sales
Natural History Museum
Cromwell Road
London SW7 5BD

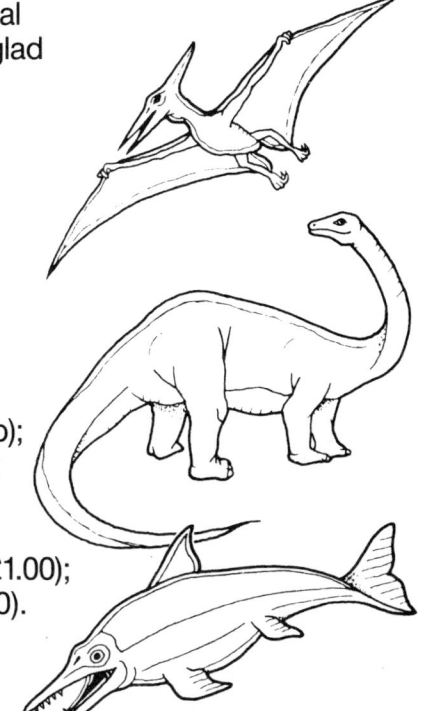

learning through doing

There are many myths and legends surrounding volcanoes.
The Romans believed that Vulcan, who was blacksmith to
the gods, worked underground on an island called Vulcano
and when the volcano there erupted they said it was Vulcan
working at his forge. The Volcanoes Acitivity Book has many
more fascinating facts as well as things to make and do and
word games to play.
Other activity books in this series are all packed with
information and games which will help you find out more about
fossils, dinosaurs, birds, insects and butterflies and moths.

directions: Use paper and an envelope. Enclose
cheque or postal order, made payable to
British Museum (Natural History), for
£1.35 for each activity book (this includes
postage and packing).

ask for: Activity books on:
Volcanoes
Fossils
Insects
Dinosaurs
Birds
Butterflies and Moths

write to: Publication Sales
Natural History Museum
Cromwell Road
London SW7 5BD

a good day for watchers

A sunny day, birds singing, bees humming – just the sort of day that WATCH members like for getting out and about. You can join WATCH whether you live in town or country because it's a club with a difference for young people who care about their surroundings. Club members get an exciting magazine, called Watchword, three times a year, full of pictures, projects, information and ideas. WATCH will send you a sample copy, and you may also ask for one of their full-colour posters.

directions: Use paper and an envelope. Enclose £1.00 cheque or postal order payable to WATCH.

ask for: Sample copy of Watchword
Full colour poster – choose from:
- Bees
- Bats
- Birds
- Ladybirds
- Streams

write to: WATCH
22 The Green
Nettleham
Lincoln LN2 2NR

help get Britain tidy

'Please take your litter home ... and help stamp out the Litter Bug', says the Tidy Britain Group. Hundreds of children are injured by broken glass. And hundreds of pets, birds, farm animals and little creatures such as mice and voles are killed and injured every day because we leave our rubbish around. It looks so ugly too. Why not get a cardboard box, stick your own poster on it and keep it in the car for the family rubbish? Send for your Litter Fighting Pack and you'll get two badges, poster and transfers, ruler, rubber, pencil and information sheets.

directions: Use paper and an envelope. Please send your name, address and cheque or postal order for £2.50 (inc. p&p) made payable to Tidy Britain Enterprises

ask for: Litter Fighting Pack

write to: The Tidy Britain Group
The Pier
Wigan WN3 4EX

you too can save a forest

It's an interesting thought that you can make a million matches out of one tree – and just one of those matches can destroy a million trees. The Forestry Commission, who protect our trees, will send you colour posters on preventing fires, and a selection of posters on forests, including their wildlife.

directions: Use paper and an envelope. Enclose the correct money (see below) and an extra large stamped addressed envelope (at least 12″ x 9″).

ask for: *Living Forest* poster (20p)
Forest-fire prevention posters (free)
How a Tree Works (free)
The Forest Code (free)
Catalogue of publications (free)

write to: Public Information Division (Schools)
The Forestry Commission
231 Corstorphine Road
Edinburgh EH12 7AT

bird in the hand

If you have ever wanted to feed the birds in your garden but haven't room for a bird table, why not try this great idea from Silverthorne. You can attract all the varieties of birds seen in and around other people's gardens to your own. These bird feeders stick onto your window and other surfaces, so you will be able to see the birds close to. Included with these bird feeders are sixteen colourful 'Spot the Bird' stickers which will help you to identify the birds when they feed. When you have spotted a bird you can place the appropriate sticker on the identification chart, which you can put up next to your window.

One point to remember is that birds take time to get used to new feeders, so be patient, but in time your patience will be rewarded and you will have regular visitors to your novelty bird table.

directions: Use paper and an envelope. Enclose a cheque or postal order for £1.66 (inc p&p).

ask for: Bird in the hand window feeder

write to: Victoria Works (FSFK offer)
Birmingham Road
Dudley
West Midlands DY1 4RL

in the country

Imagine you are in the heart of the English countryside with these gifts and activity sheets from the Cotswold Countryside Collection at Northleach. There are four colouring sheets, a choice of four delightful brooches, pens, bookmarks and some posters to decorate your wall.

directions: Use paper and an envelope. Enclose cheque or postal order for the correct amount.

ask for: Colouring sheets (£1.05 each) of:
Shire horses of England;
Shepherd in the springtime;
Wildlife in a cornfield;
Bringing in the harvest.
Wooden animal brooch (£1.05 each) of:
Frog   Owl
Mouse   Pig
Posters (65p each) of:
Shire horses   Harvest mice
Dormouse   Barn owls
Bookmark (70p)
Pen (55p)

write to: Cotswold Countryside Collection
Northleach
Cheltenham
Glos. GL54 3JH

birds to colour

If you borrow a bird book from the library you will know exactly how to colour these birds accurately. It will help you spot the birds in the wild, too.

directions: Use paper and an envelope. Enclose 75p (postal order or cheque) for 1 poster or £1.40 for 2.

ask for: Garden birds   Sea birds
Meadowland birds   British birds

write to: The Comenius Company Ltd
17 Castle View Park
Mawnan Smith
Falmouth, Cornwall

a is for anteater

This lovely ABC colouring book is not just for young ones learning to read. Anyone who enjoys colouring a well-drawn picture will spend hours of fun with the animals, birds and other creatures found here.

directions: Use paper and an envelope. Enclose cheque or postal order, made payable to British Museum (Natural History), for £1.35.

ask for: ABC colouring book

write to: Publication Sales
Natural History Museum
Cromwell Road, London SW7 5BD

growing wild flowers

By planning a wild flower garden you will be helping birds, bees, butterflies, moths and a variety of insects. This leaflet from the Royal Society for Nature Conservation will get you started.

directions: Use paper and an envelope. Enclose 6" x 9" stamped addressed envelope.

ask for: Focus on Wild Flower Gardening

write to: RSNC, The Green
Nettleham, Lincoln LN2 2NR

birds in your garden

Can you recognise all the birds that come into your garden? This full-colour booklet Discover Garden Birds has illustrations of the ones most commonly seen with notes on what food you can put out for them and advice on how to attract different birds to your garden. The Young Ornithologists' Club will also send you membership details of their club and a large colour poster all about kestrels.

directions: Use paper and an envelope. Please send 2 first class stamps.

ask for: Discover Garden Birds booklet
Kestrel poster; YOC membership details

write to: Young Ornithologists' Club (FSFK/2)
RSPB, The Lodge
Sandy
Bedfordshire SG19 2DL

protect your world

And this pack will help you to do it. It has lots of information plus a colouring book, poster, sticker, badge, notelet, pen and pencil. The pack tells you how to make your own paper, grow a tree from seed and much more.

directions: Use a paper and an envelope. Please enclose a self-addressed label with a 30p stamp plus £1.73.

ask for: Young Supporter's Pack

write to: Conservation Trust, George Palmer Site
Northumberland Avenue
Reading, Berks RG2 7PW

magnify a mollusc

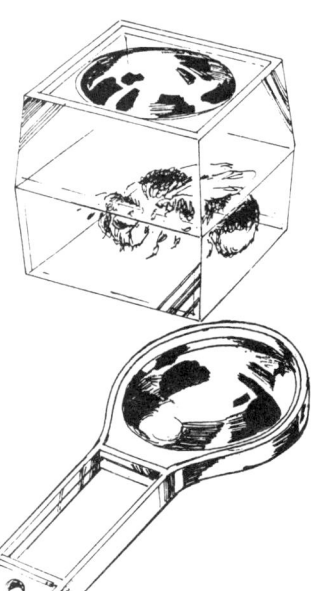

How many times have you wanted to study an insect closely only to have it jump out of your hand? What you need is a bug-box then you can put your chosen beetle or other crawly thing in the box and look at it through the magnifying lid. Don't forget to let it go again, though. You can use the box to examine flowers, leaves and seeds, too.

directions: Use paper and an envelope. Enclose postal order or cheque for £1.65.

ask for: Bug Box

write to: Bug Box of Cornwall
17 Castle View Park
Mawnan Smith
Falmouth, Cornwall

animals in the countryside

If you enjoy colouring, then you'll love these packs of four colouring sheets from the Cotswold Countryside Collection. The Farmyard pack has a Rhode Island Red cockerel, a Guernsey cow and calf, a Dorset Horn sheep and a Wessex Saddleback pig with piglets. The British Mammals pack has a rabbit, red fox, badger and the rather rare red squirrel. Each pack contains a colour guide to help you paint or colour a really authentic picture and if you do them carefully you could mount them on coloured card afterwards and hang the set of four on your wall.

directions: Use paper and an envelope. Enclose £1.20 for each pack you want.

ask for: Farmyard colouring pack
British Mammals colouring pack

write to: Cotswold Countryside Collection
Northleach
Cheltenham
Glos GL54 3JH

HAVE YOU READ THE DIRECTIONS CAREFULLY?

**NATURE &
CONSERVATION**

secrets of nature

Have a guess at how many earthworms there are in a field.
Could there be 500? Or 5,000? Or 500,000? The true and
staggering answer is that, in a hectare of old pasture, there
could be as many as 7.2 million! This full-colour wallchart has
more facts about life on the grasslands, uplands, woodland,
farmland, in the towns, on the seashore and in the water.
For instance, did you know that although most of our
hedgerows date from the 18th and 19th centuries, some of
them go back to Saxon times? You can roughly date a hedge
by counting each different kind of tree and bush in a 30 metre
stretch and multiplying the number of species by 100. This
gives the approximate age of the hedge in years. This wallchart
is included in a special pack put together by the Nature
Conservancy Council and also includes a *Get to Know Nature*
booklet, a nature jotter and a colour catalogue.

directions: Use paper and an envelope. Enclose
a cheque or postal order for £1.99.

ask for: *Secrets of Nature* wallchart
Get to Know Nature booklet
Nature jotter
Colour catalogue

write to: Dept DO, Publications
Nature Conservancy Council
Northminster House
Peterborough PE1 1UA

nature in your town

This beautifully illustrated nature discovery book shows you where to find wildlife in towns, how to make a nature map, carry out weather, soil and flower studies, 'adopt a tree', collect bark patterns and plaster casts and watch for creatures of the night. Even walls, pavements and stones have secrets to tell.

directions: Use paper and an envelope. Enclose a cheque or postal order for £1.95 (a special price for FREE STUFF readers)

ask for: Nature in your Town

write to: Dept. FS, Humane Education Centre
Avenue Lodge
Bounds Green Road, London N22 4EU

all living things

If you care about animals, write off for a free copy of 'All Living Things', the magazine of the Young Crusaders, the junior section of the Crusade Against All Cruelty to Animals.

directions: Use paper and an envelope. Please enclose a long s.a.e.

ask for: All Living Things

write to: Dept. FS, Humane Education Centre
Avenue Lodge
Bounds Green Road
London N22 4EU

for animal lovers

Find out about animals with the RSPCA. *Animal World* is the magazine for Junior Members and is full of articles, stories, photographs, drawings, quizzes, cartoons, activities and information on a whole range of animal welfare topics. And you can now send for a FREE complimentary copy of this magazine. This organisation cares for the welfare of all animals, both domesticated and those that live in the wild. You can also receive details of the RSPCA Junior Membership Scheme which is open to anyone aged up to 17 years. If you then decide to become a member you will be joining with the many thousands of young people who care about animals.

directions: Use a postcard

ask for: A complimentary copy of *Animal World*

write to: Junior Membership Dept (FSFK)
RSPCA
Causeway
Horsham
West Sussex
RH12 1HG

help a hedgehog

Hedgehogs really do have quite a hard life. They have to cross roads where cars are hurtling past at 50 or 60 miles an hour. Then, when they heave a sigh of relief at getting into someone's quiet garden, it isn't even safe there. Poisonous pellets, put down for slugs, can also kill hedgehogs, ponds are a danger to them and hedgehogs have even been known to become entangled in tennis nets where they starve to death.

The hedgehog is the gardener's friend – it will eat slugs, beetles and caterpillars, so should be encouraged.

If you would like to know how to help the hedgehog, write to the British Hedgehog Preservation Society who will send you a leaflet about hedgehogs, another leaflet explaining the work of the Society and a catalogue of the goods they have for sale.

directions: Use paper and an envelope. Enclose a stamped addressed envelope 9″ x 6½″.

ask for: Explanatory leaflet about the Society
Leaflet about hedgehogs
Catalogue

write to: British Hedgehog Preservation Society
Knowbury House
Knowbury
Ludlow
Shropshire SY8 3LQ

going ... going ... gone?

Have you heard about the rain forest in Brazil? Have you heard how it's disappearing fast? Do you know that people are trying to save it? This isn't a problem just of trees or climate, it also means the loss of a way of life for the people who live there. This free material from Christian Aid includes a game illustrating why the rain forests are being cut down, information about Brazil, an hilarious animal song and a 12-page booklet, with pictures to colour, telling the story of a family, some donkeys and a battle to save a forest home.

directions: Use a postcard. Don't forget to include your name and address.

ask for: Going ... going ... gone?

write to:

Ann Giles
Dept F
Education Sector
Christian Aid
P.O. Box 100
London SE1 7RT

help win the war on want

War on Want is a charity fighting a war on world poverty and you can help them. Send off for this information pack, which is free, but if you also send a donation (postal order or cheque), however small, you will be helping people less fortunate than yourself.

directions: Use paper and an envelope. Enclose a large s.a.e. stamped with 28p.

ask for: Free Stuff for Kids pack, including information material, a badge, stickers, a balloon and a poster.

write to: Jo White, War on Want
37-39 Great Guildford Street
London SE1 0ES

the Badgers are coming ...

And if you're aged between 6 and 10 you can join the Badgers, too. It is the junior section of St John Ambulance and members wear a simple uniform, belong to their own Badger Set and take part in a vast range of activities including picnics, parties, games, sports and a training scheme.

directions: Use a postcard

ask for: Free information about the Badgers

write to: Sarah Harris, Badgers Free Stuff
St John Ambulance Headquarters
1 Grosvenor Crescent
London SW1X 7EF

children first

UNICEF – the United Nations' Children's Fund – works to help children in 118 countries around the world. Its magazine Children First has up to the minute news from many of these countries and also tells you how local organisations are helping too. UNICEF wants to give children everywhere the chance to drink clean water, eat enough food and be protected against killer diseases. You can also send for a poster and a leaflet telling the story of UNICEF in words and pictures. Recently a BBC team and UNICEF workers travelled to Nepal to report on that country and this Nepal Pack resulted from that visit.

directions: Use paper and an envelope. Enclose a large (A4) self-addressed envelope, stamped with 24p.

ask for: Children First magazine
The Story of UNICEF leaflet
UNICEF poster
Nepal Pack

write to: Information Officer
UNICEF-UK
55 Lincolns Inn Fields
London WC2A 3NB

lucky ladybirds

The Pestalozzi Village, now set in the beautiful Sussex countryside, was started in Switzerland many years ago to look after war-orphaned children. This British Village now cares for children from the poorer countries where people often go hungry. You can help by sending for this Pestalozzi package which has the lucky ladybird emblem on both badges.

directions: Use paper and an envelope. Please send postal order or cheque for £1.00.

ask for: Pestalozzi pen, Ladybird button badge and leaflet.

write to: The Appeals Administrator
Dept FSFK, Pestalozzi Children's Village
Sedlescombe, East Sussex TN33 0RR

Red Cross Youth

Members of the Red Cross are often seen at fêtes giving first aid, but do you know anything else about the Society? Maybe you'd like to become a member? This free colour leaflet has details of some of the wonderful work it does both in this country and abroad.

directions: Use a postcard

ask for: Meet the Red Cross booklet

write to: Youth Dept., British Red Cross Society
9 Grosvenor Crescent, London SW1

a friend in need

Over 120 years ago, Dr Thomas Barnardo gave destitute children in London homes and hope amongst the poverty and cruelty of the life they knew.

Today Barnardo's helps more than 16,000 young people through a network of schools and community-based projects across Britain. Barnardo's works with young people who have mental and physical handicaps, who face social or emotional deprivation, or whose families need help and support. Write to Barnardo's for a comic which tells you about the Barnardo's story. They will also send you a snazzy hat, leaflets, a booklet of photographs and a car sticker.

directions: Use paper and an envelope. Send your name and full address plus 60p in stamps.

ask for: Free Stuff for Kids

write to: The Information Officer
Publicity Section
Barnardo's
Tanners Lane
Barkingside
Essex EG6 1QG

sight savers

Sight Savers is an organisation run by the Royal Commonwealth Society for the Blind. They work only in Third World countries. In India, Pakistan, Bangladesh and Sri Lanka they have set up eye camps where people can go and have their sight tested and if an operation is needed they can do that too.

In Africa they are providing braille books to help blind children learn in the classrooms of ordinary schools. They also buy braille games, dominoes, playing cards and crossword puzzles, in fact most things that sighted children have in *their* schools.

If you send for the Sight Savers 'Kids pack' you will get more information about their good work plus a balloon, badge, sticker, a braille alphabet, a message in braille and a 'savie', which is a reflective sticker for you to put on your clothes or bag so you can be seen by drivers in the dark.

directions: Use paper and an envelope. Enclose 50p postal order.

ask for: 'Kids pack'

write to: Information Services (Ref: JLW)
Sight Savers
Royal Commonwealth Society for the Blind
Commonwealth House
Haywards Heath RH16 3AZ

meeting blind people

Some people feel nervous or embarrassed when they meet a blind person. They don't know what to say, so they address all their remarks to a companion. This leaflet has all the answers to the problem, but the main message is, 'behave naturally'.

directions: Use paper and an envelope. Enclose a 9½" x 6½" s.a.e.

ask for: Meeting blind people

write to: Community Education Officer, RNIB
224 Great Portland Street
London W1N 6AA

fingerspelling

When you are talking to a deaf person, he or she can often lipread if you speak slowly and clearly. Sometimes, though, it's useful to know sign language so that you can spell out words that are difficult to understand. This fingerspelling card will teach you how to form the alphabet.

directions: Use paper and an envelope. Enclose a second-class stamp.

ask for: Fingerspelling card

write to: Royal Association in Aid of Deaf People
27 Old Oak Road, London W3 7HN

try, try, try again

When King Robert the Bruce of Scotland was hiding from the English in a cave, he watched a spider try again and again until it bridged a gap to weave its web. Encouraged by this example, Bruce defeated the English at the famous battle of Bannockburn. Today the National Trust for Scotland have produced an exciting show at the Bannockburn Heritage Centre which recreates the battle. You can see King Robert cleave an English knight's skull in two with his battle axe and hear the clash of arms during the battle! You get free entry to this show with the ticket below and if you write to the Trust, they will send you details of over 100 exciting visits in Scotland.

directions: Use paper and an envelope. Enclose 6″ x 8″ stamped addressed envelope

ask for: Free information about over 100 National Trust for Scotland properties

write to: Merchandising Dept.
The National Trust for Scotland
5 Charlotte Square
Edinburgh
EH2 4DU

**AUDIO VISUAL SHOW
BANNOCKBURN**

Bannockburn Heritage Centre
Glasgow Road
Stirling FK7 0LJ

Admit one child under 14 FREE, when accompanied by a paying adult.

lighthouses

The shipwrecked mariner would never have been in such distress if he'd had a cheery light beaming out into the night warning of treacherous seas and rocks. Today there are over 190 lighthouses around the Scottish and Manx coastlines. Some of these are open to the public and make exciting places to visit. For a list of lighthouses in Scotland and the Isle of Man and diagrams about how they work write to the Northern Lighthouse Board.

directions: Use paper and an envelope. Enclose a first class stamp.

ask for: Diagrams and list of lighthouses in Scotland and the Isle of Man

write to: Administration Officer
Northern Lighthouse Board
84 George Street, Edinburgh EH2 3DA

Why not send off for information about the lighthouses off the coast of England and Wales – plus the work of Trinity House, London?

directions: Use paper and an envelope. Please enclose a large stamped addressed envelope.

ask for: Information about Trinity House

write to: Information Officer
Corporation of Trinity House
Trinity House
Tower Hill, London EC3N 4DH

how far can you see?

This series of panoramas will show you just what you can expect to see after you've panted your way to the top of one of the mountains mentioned below.

directions: Use paper and an envelope. Enclose a postal order for each panorama you want and a large s.a.e.

ask for: Panorama from: Ben Nevis (90p) Snowdon (55p), Snaefell (80p) or Glastonbury Tor (40p)

write to: Jesty's Panoramas, Sunlyn Allington Park Bridport, Dorset DT6 5DD

a lovely day out

London for Kids is an 80-page magazine absolutely packed with details of all the most interesting places to visit, not only in London, but for some forty miles around. There are museums, parks, nature trails, farms, railways, aeroplanes, zoos, safari parks, river and canal trips, seaside resorts and sports activities. All you have to do is choose where to go first!

directions: Use paper and an envelope. Enclose £1.00 plus 50p postage and packing.

ask for: a copy of *London for Kids*

write to: R.P.L., 312A High Road London E10 5PW

DON'T SEND COINS OR STAMPS UNLESS YOU ARE ASKED TO DO SO.

discover England

If you and your family can't decide where to go for your holiday this year why not ask the English Tourist Board for some free information to help you make up your mind?

directions: Use a postcard

ask for: Information on English holidays, short breaks, Tourist Information Centres, miniature and model villages, safari and wildlife parks.

write to: ETB Correspondence Dept
Thames Tower, Blacks Road
Hammersmith, London W6 9EL

discover Scotland

Scotland's a surprising place. It has castles, caves, stone circles, abbeys, towers, lochs, gardens and glens. There are palm-fringed beaches, wildlife parks, butterfly farms and pleasure cruises. To find out more about holidays in Surprising Scotland, send for this free brochure.

directions: Use a postcard

ask for: Scotland – It's a Different Holiday Every Day; Scotland Welcomes Children

write to: The Scottish Tourist Board
PO Box 705
Edinburgh EH4 3EU

discover Wales

Wales offers you several different kinds of holiday. If you like visiting castles there are really spectacular ones like Beaumaris, Caernarfon, Conwy and Harlech. But if you prefer the seaside there are miles of beaches, while the energetic ones can plump for an activity holiday. These brochures will give you all the information you need.

directions: Use a postcard

ask for: Wales Brochure
Activity Holidays Series

write to: Wales Tourist Board, Dept FSFK
PO Box 1, Cardiff CF1 2XN

discover N. Ireland

The Giant's Causeway in Northern Ireland is world-famous for its 40,000 many-sided stone columns. There are lots more attractions to be found here and this mini-guide will help you plan an Irish holiday to remember.

directions: Use a postcard

ask for: Northern Ireland mini-guide

write to: Tourist Information Office
River House, 48 High Street
Belfast BT1 2DS

a hostel holiday

Youth hostelling is an inexpensive and fun way of taking a holiday. The Youth Hostels Association has 260 Hostels in cities, towns, at the seaside, in National Parks, on long distance paths – in fact, wherever people like to go for holidays. It has over a quarter of a million members in England and Wales who like cycling, walking or touring around meeting other people and having a wonderful holiday at the same time. This free YHA Accommodation Guide will tell you where the Hostels are and how you and your family can become members.

directions: Use paper and an envelope. Enclose self-addressed envelope (10″ x 7″), stamped with 30p.

ask for: YHA Accommodation Guide (England and Wales)

write to: Marketing Services
Youth Hostels Association
Trevelyan House
8 St Stephen's Hill
St Albans
Herts AL1 2DY

flour power

Q: What have the following in common: Vienna, Danish, split tin, plait, barrel, bloomer, coburg, cottage, farmhouse and cob? A: They're all different shapes of bread that you could find in any baker's shop in your local High Street. These leaflets from the Flour Advisory Bureau are packed with information to make us more knowledgeable about a product that most households use every day. For instance, did you know that bread is one of the oldest foods known to man and has been an important food for over 5,000 years; or that in Ancient Egyptian times, officials were paid with it?

Whether you're doing a project or just want to know more about flour, these leaflets make interesting reading and the packed meals fact sheet has lots of ideas for making lunch-time sandwiches really different.

directions: Use paper and an envelope. Enclose 19p stamp and your name and address.

ask for: Fact sheets on: Packed Meals for Schoolchildren; Flour; Flour Milling; The Story of Bread; Know your Wheatgrain; Wake up to Bread Poster; Bread for Healthy Living.

write to: Ref. EX1
Flour Advisory Bureau
21 Arlington Street
London SW1A 1RN

Britain and Europe

Do you know what really goes on in Parliament? These publications will help. There's a booklet called *The Palace of Westminster* for the under 12s and education sheets for the over 13s.

directions: Use a postcard

ask for: Education sheets on Parliament
OR The Palace of Westminster

write to: The Parliamentary Education Unit
Room 507, Norman Shaw (South) Building
Victoria Embankment, London SW1A 0AA

Send for these free publications and you'll be a lot wiser about the European Parliament. It makes excellent project material for the over 10s and teachers would no doubt be interested in the other material listed below.

directions: Use a postcard.

ask for: European Parliament news (monthly)
European Parliament Brochure – One
    Parliament for Twelve
European Parliament Leaflet
Poster, stickers and postcard
Study Card
VHS Video (for teachers) *010 for Europe*

write to: Dept FSK, European Parliament
2 Queen Anne's Gate
London SW1H 9AA

Greenscene

More than a quarter of a million people every year are becoming vegetarians. They don't eat meat, but get their protein from things like nuts, cheese, eggs and beans. What do you think about vegetarianism? Perhaps your teacher would like to do a project on it. If so, this material from the Vegetarian Society would make a good talking point. It is more suitable for older children.

directions: Use paper and an envelope. Enclose the correct money and 2 first-class stamps.

ask for: Free leaflets and stickers
A-Z of Vegetarianism (50p)
Greenscene magazine (50p – special price for FSFK readers)

write to: Youth Dept, The Vegetarian Society
Parkdale, Dunham Road
Altrincham, Cheshire WA14 4QG

what's an E number?

Find out more about the soft drinks industry and what additives and E numbers are by sending off for this free information.

directions: Use a postcard

ask for: Materials and information on soft drinks and additives

write to: British Soft Drinks Association
6 Catherine Street, London WC2B 5UA

farming today

Been set a project about farming at school? Or simply want to know more about where your food comes from?
The NFU, which represents farmers and growers in England and Wales, has set up a Farming Information Centre which carries a wide range of leaflets and information about British farming.

directions: Use paper and an envelope. Enclose a stamped, addressed envelope 10" x 7".

ask for: Publications list

write to: NFU Farming Information Centre
Agriculture House
Knightsbridge, London SW1X 7NJ

calling all smokebusters!

If you want to grow up to be strong and healthy you and your friends should grow up as nonsmokers – people who never smoke cigarettes. Being a nonsmoker can be fun. Wear your very own "I am a smoke-free zone" badge.

directions: Use paper and an envelope. Enclose a large s.a.e. stamped with 30p plus cheque or postal order made payable to ASH.

ask for: 'I am a smoke-free zone' badge (25p)
Slinger pen (99p)
Project pack with sticker (free)

write to: Action on Smoking and Health (FSFK)
5/11 Mortimer Street, London W1N 7RH

index

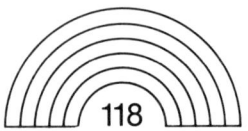

Other interesting books from EXLEY

In the same series:

Rainy Day Fun and Games. *£7.99 (hardback).* With over 100 things to make or do, children will actually look forward to a rainy day with this book in the house. There are so many different ideas: why not grow your own plants indoors, make something delicious to eat, build a landscape for your dinosaurs, puzzle your friends with some magic, or try one of the many card or party games. You needn't even wait for the rain to start having fun.

Sing As We Go. *£7.99 (hardback).* A collection of one hundred really popular songs for the family or school to sing on journeys, sing-songs or other times when you need to amuse yourselves. You should know the tunes for practically all these standard favourites.

Play As We Go. *£7.99 (hardback).* Most parents dread taking children on long journeys because of the boredom factor. However, with this book to hand, this should never be a problem again! Packed with games and small-scale activities for children ranging from three to thirteen, this should keep them amused for hours and prevent fraying tempers all round.

Other Titles:

Crafty Ideas From Nature. *£7.99 (hardback).* The first title in a new series for young children, which stresses "learning by doing" – and having fun at the same time. Packed full of good ideas for things to make and do using natural products, there are over 40 projects ranging from making floral notepaper, through jewellery and presents, to growing a miniature garden and some fun board games. Illustrated throughout in full colour and with step-by-step instuctions, all these projects have been tried out by parents and teachers of children in the first years at school. This book has been authored by Myrna Daitz and Shirley Williams, both parents and schoolteachers, while Gillian Chapman has illustrated several top-selling early-learning books.

Watch out for the next titles in the series, coming in 1990: **Crafty Ideas From Junk** and **Crafty Ideas For Presents.**

PEOPLE WHO HAVE HELPED THE WORLD: This important new series of biographies for children aged eleven to fourteen has been acclaimed as one of the best biography series to have been produced for years. Illustrated throughout in colour and black-and-white, in hardback, they cost £5.99 each. The first twelve titles are now available in a handsome slipcase at the special price of £60.00 (a saving of £11.88!).

Titles published or in preparation include: **Robert Baden Powell / Louis Braille / Marie Curie / The Dalai Lama / Father Damien / Henry Dunant / Mahatma Gandhi / Bob Geldof / Martin Luther King / Maria Montessori / Florence Nightingale / Louis Pasteur / Sir Peter Scott / Albert Schweitzer / Mother Teresa / Desmond Tutu / Lech Walesa / Raoul Wallenberg**

These books make super presents. Order them from your local bookseller or from Exley Publications Ltd, Dept BP, 16 Chalk Hill, Watford, Herts WD1 4BN. (Please send £1.00 to cover post and packing.) Exley Publications reserves the right to show new retail prices on books which may vary from those previously advertised.